Universal Design For Safety

Creating Safe & Accessible Living Spaces For All Ages

Universal Design For Safety

Creating Safe & Accessible Living Spaces For All Ages

Steve Hoffacker

AICP, CAASH, CAPS, CGA, CGP, CMP, CSP, MCSP, MIRM

Universal Design For Safety

Creating Safe & Accessible Living Spaces For All Ages

Cover photo by Steve Hoffacker.

ALL RIGHTS RESERVED.

―――

They say that a person's homes is their castle. Therefore, it should be the safest place we can go. Universal design solutions and treatments make sure that safety is a prime objective in creating fun, enjoyable, peaceful, and comfortable living spaces where we can return to shut out the outside world. There are so many perils waiting for us in the world that we need to have the peace-of-mind that our homes afford us relative safety. There still are many accidents that occur in the home, but the design elements we use should not contribute to them or cause them.

―――

Other Sales Content
By Steve Hoffacker

To access or learn about books, eBooks, articles, blogs, commentary, and other content by Steve Hoffacker for anyone who sells products or services for a living, use the sites below.

"Hoffacker Associates" Website
http://stevehoffacker.com

Steve Hoffacker's Amazon.com Author Page
http://amazon.com/author/stevehoffacker

"Steve Hoffacker's Home Sales Insights" Blog
http://homesalesinsights.com

"Steve Hoffacker's Sales Quips" Blog
http://salesquips.com

"Steve Hoffacker's Success Quips" Blog
http://successquips.com

Steve Hoffacker and Hoffacker Associates can be found online at Facebook, Active Rain, Pinterest, Linked-In, Plaxo, Twitter, Goggle+, YouTube, Tumblr, and other business, real estate, and social sites.

Table Of Contents

Preface

Like many of my books, this text is available in both printed and Kindle eBook editions.

Both versions are similar in content although there are formatting differences between them.

This book is another in my series on universal design — "Common Sense Universal Design," "Universal Design For Builders," and "Universal Design And Aging" are the others — so far.

They aren't a series in the sense that they continue from one to another — just that they all deal with various aspects of universal design. Some of the material is similar or possibly the same in each book, but the emphasis and focus is different depending on the title and how the material is intended to be used.

Universal design is concerned with making living spaces as usable and accessible as possible for anyone in the home, regardless of their age or physical ability.

The book you are reading now concentrates on the safety aspects of selecting the appropriate design so that our homes are as comfortable as possible.

This book has a general audience in mind. Both the consumer and the professional should find that it is a great resource and handbook for evaluating changes that can be made in anyone's home — regardless of their present age and who does the renovations.

This book, like the one I wrote on aging ("Universal Design And Aging") will describe available lifestyle choices for people as they remain in their homes, but it will focus even more on the safety aspects of the renovations and improvements that can be made.

Similarly, a safety emphasis for any age or ability will use material from "Common Sense Universal Design" and "Universal Design For Builders" and then expand upon it.

Certainly homeowners will benefit from the safety aspects of universal design usage, but renters (in an apartment building, condo building, or free-standing home) and apartment building owners or managers will as well.

Regardless of how the changes are accomplished — by the homeowner, renter, building owner, or paid professional — the information in this book describes many improvements, treatments, renovations, and solutions to living spaces in general that will add to the comfort, enjoyment, and overall safety in anyone's home.

A remodeler, contractor, handyman, occupational therapist, interior designer, kitchen and bath designer, flooring contractor, HVAC contractor, DME (durable medical equipment) supplier, electrical services contractor (ESC), and so many others are capable of providing specialized assistance to make any living space functional, comfortable, and safe — regardless of anyone's age or physical ability.

There are so many opportunities to swap out or exchange existing features, fixtures, devices, and accessories with something more appropriate in terms of accessibility, comfort, convenience, and safety — or to modify existing spaces to create those opportunities — regardless of who is doing the work.

While universal design concepts accommodate all ages, there is a real opportunity to create designs that appeal to safe and comfortable living spaces for seniors and those remaining in their homes over time.

As you might know, I base my recommendations and suggestions on several years (and counting) of teaching the Certified Aging-in-Place Specialist ("CAPS") designation program through the National Association of Home Builders, the interactions and contributions of the hundreds of attendees at these programs, my independent research and earlier books, and the remodeling I have done on my own homes using such products and solutions.

I have no formal training in architecture or design other than the experience gained in teaching the CAPS program and more than 3 decades of consulting with homebuilders.

Nevertheless, the concepts I discuss in this text have been validated by personal experience in the remodeling of my own homes, focus groups with new home buyers over the years, and the concurrence and input of hundreds of attendees at my programs — as well as the great reception for my other universal design books.

You'll find as you read what I have prepared for you that universal design is an intuitive approach that works as an effective solution and strategy for many living environments — especially as a great way to make our homes continue to serve us well as we age.

In fact, there are few homes anywhere that couldn't benefit from the use and application of these principles — unless they were designed that way to begin with or have already been modified.

This is not a concept that is just for the United States, or for Canada, or even North America. This can be applied to homes anywhere in the world.

While the traditional universal design approach accommodates a tremendous range of ages, heights, and physical abilities, our main focus in this text is how those treatments promote safety in the living space.

Even for specific physical needs that might require more particular design emphasis and solutions than universal design affords, universal design is still an integral part of the overall approach and a great place to begin because it already allows for a range of heights and physical abilities.

While the ideas and strategies presented here are based on technology and solutions currently available, it is entirely likely that new products and solutions or even best practices will become available that meet the definition and spirit of universal design and how it is delivered that should be considered for use as they become known.

Universal design can help you establish safer living environments with virtually invisible changes — by adding new elements or replacing existing features and components with more accessible ones. When completed, the features and concepts shouldn't look much different from what they are replacing.

If visitors to someone's home don't specifically know what they are looking at and what has been replaced, they will think that what they see is just a creative part of the design.

The key to successful home modifications using universal design is making improvements that are essentially invisible — ones that do not call attention to themselves.

There are specific design solutions that can be accomplished for wheelchair access, but universal design solutions accommodate those in most cases and don't suggest how or by whom the space is to be used.

This book is not intended to address every single area of the home but will provide many solid ideas and strategies on ways to make nearly anyone's home more accessible, comfortable, attractive, convenient, serviceable, functional, and safe as people want an immediate solution now, want to make their homes more attractive and saleable, or want to continue living in them for many years.

Universal design is a great concept for both interior and exterior treatments. Done with a focus on safety, it becomes even more powerful.

Universal Design For Safety

Creating Safe & Accessible Living Spaces For All Ages

1

Universal Design Promotes Safety

The Importance Of Safety

There are so many challenges to our personal safety as we are away from home and out in the workplace or marketplace.

We are at risk as we drive our cars or travel by train, bus, ferry, or plane.

We run the risk of being attacked or accosted by someone else.

We can stumble on sidewalks or stepping off curbs. We can be hit by various objects as they are propelled by the wind. We can be served bad food.

It may not even be a personal attack or direct threat on our property that concerns us but just a general uneasiness or worry about being places where so much can happen to us.

There are so many ways — many more than I have just briefly mentioned — that we can feel insecure or at risk when we are away from home. Therefore, we look forward to returning to the relative safety of our homes after a day at the office, one or more days traveling, or even a trip to the market or shopping.

Safety at home isn't guaranteed. We have to work at it. Some home are better equipped to provide it than others. Still, there are measures that we can take to improve the overall safety, security, and peace-of-mind we enjoy while in the comfort of our home and yard or setting.

In this book, we are going to look at universal design as a strategy for promoting safer, more enjoyable living spaces — whether you are a homeowner or tenant. We'll begin with an understanding of what universal design is — and what it is not.

How Universal Design Fits In

As we look at and explore why universal design promotes safer, more enjoyable living spaces — whether someone is a homeowner or tenant, we have to begin with an understanding of what universal design is — and what it is not.

Universal design is a concept, treatment, solution, or strategy — depending on how and when it is applied to the living space — that results in safe, convenient, comfortable, accessible, friendly, desirable, visitable, marketable, sustainable, and serviceable living areas for anyone — regardless of their age, physical ability, height, dexterity, coordination, or other attributes.

No one has to wait for a certain time in their life before employing universal design treatments or solutions. They can be used at any point in one's lifetime — especially with the emphasis on safety.

There is no magical time or event that has to happen first before universal design improvements can or should be done or undertaken — or where they would be appreciated or considered more appropriate than at an earlier time in someone's life.

Similarly, the concept of "aging-in-place" which is closely aligned to universal design is not event or age related either.

While universal design has some particularly great applications for people as they age, it doesn't have to wait to be applied until later in life. It works quite well for families with young children, single-person households, and homes with several people of differing ages, sizes, and abilities — as well as everything else in between. It is indifferent to someone's age.

Universal design — because of what it is and what it promotes — works for people in any age group and regardless of how many people may be sharing the same living space, from one person on up.

It also applies regardless of someone's physical size or ability.

That's why it is labeled "universal." It works for nearly everyone in any situation — even people that might have special mobility, sensory, or cognitive needs or concerns.

It is a great strategy to make anyone's home safer at any stage of their life, and it promotes the concept of aging-in-place safely and effectively as the years pass.

Exploring Universal Design

Perhaps you have some idea of what universal design is, or it might just be a term that you have heard of but would be stuck on trying to define it.

Let me provide a simple, yet comprehensive, definition of the concept of universal design and why it works so well for people of any age.

Essentially, universal design means that anyone of any age or ability living in any home — or visiting them in that residence, whether for a couple of hours or for several days — can have equal access to any part of that home, inside and out, and enjoy success in using the various features, fixtures, appliances, and controls in it without any special knowledge, compensation, or consideration. This is why it works so well for anyone who wants their homes to continue serving them well as they live in them long-term and grow older.

It also means that your guests or visitors would feel as welcome as you in your home and quite comfortable getting around in your home — whether their visit is just for a few hours or it's an extended stay for several days or even months.

Being able to navigate through someone's home or access switches, doors, drawers, windows, faucets, and other facilities, fixtures, or devices would be comfortable and convenient for anyone to use — whether they are the normal occupant of that home (regardless of their age) or a visitor or guest.

No special physical size, height, coordination, or physical ability would be required. This is the beauty of universal design.

It makes sense and it offers a very practical solution and strategy for increasing the safety, comfort, convenience, and accessibility for everyone, regardless of what type of living space it is. It eliminates over-reaching, strain, and exertion.

This is the real deal. There is nothing trendy or faddish about it. Even without labeling it "universal design," the concepts are just something you would want to include in a renovation project to create a safe environment.

It makes sense and offers practical, comfortable, intuitive, accessible, unobtrusive, and contemporary solutions and styles in addition to enhancing safety.

Recognizing Universal Design

Essentially, universal design — whether a product, fixture, feature, renovation, improvement, treatment, concept, or strategy — must appeal to and be usable and accessible to the general population without qualification. That's what makes it universal.

We are particularly interested in how it can make life easier and simpler — and of course safer — for anyone.

Regardless of our current age — young or old — safety is of the utmost value to us in our homes. As we age and remain in our homes, it becomes that much more important. Nevertheless, living in our homes should be enjoyable and safe at any age.

With the possible exception of those individuals that require specific design applications for their particular mobility needs and physical abilities, universal design generally serves quite well for the normal aging process (at whatever age someone happens to be at the moment) and for those who have various special access needs or requirements.

Using universal design treatments and features does not demand any advance knowledge or instruction in how to operate something (such as turning on a faucet or light switch, or opening a door).

In addition, the solutions and fixtures must be so easy and flexible or forgiving to use that a person doesn't have to operate them perfectly or "just-so" in order to make them work effectively.

They must be installed or located so that nearly anyone can reach and use them — from small to tall, as well as a seated, kneeling, or standing position.

Over time as we get older, we may lose some of our hand or arm strength, stamina, or the physical flexibility of standing as upright or reaching or bending from the waist or knees as easily as we once did.

Thus, universal applications and concepts contribute the overall safety and comfort of living in one's home and being able to use all the facets of it enjoyably and successfully.

Using universal design treatments should require a minimum of effort and not depend on any particular height, hand or arm strength, gripping or grasping ability, or range-of-motion.

Small children, tall teenagers and adults, average size individuals, or those with restrictions concerning reach, strength, or standing should still be able to access, reach, and operate the controls in a home.

When used correctly and appropriately, universal design elements fit seamlessly into the living space and become just part of the home without calling attention to the design or sticking out in anyway as something special or unusual.

Being unobtrusive is a major design objective.

Universal Design Works

In addition to just fitting into any home without being obvious that a design change has occurred, universal design features actually enhance the appearance, value, comfort, and safety of those homes.

This is why universal design is desired and why it works.

Putting in such items as single-lever faucets, lever door handles, or rocker light switches makes living spaces safer for us, makes the controls easier to operate, makes it more convenient for anyone to use, and adds value to our homes since people interested in purchasing them at a later date would look for, expect to find, and appreciate such features being already included.

Thus, our homes will look more attractive, more inviting (for guests or visitors to come to our homes and feel welcome), safer, more convenient, more comfortable, and more contemporary (with up-to-date features).

These features don't need to be updated as we age or remain in our homes — or as our homes are sold. That's the great part about installing them now. They are relatively timeless because they work so well.

Also, universal design features and improvements contribute to our sense of well-being in living in our homes and managing the living environment.

Whether someone is living in their first home, the home where they have raised their children and seen them go on to form their own households and families, or a home that can be considered the ideal home to remain in for one's mature years, universal design can help make that home safer, more comfortable, more usable, and contribute to the overall quality of life.

The key the is to find a home or adapt it so that it provides the maximum safety for peace-of-mind, security, convenience, and comfortable living.

So many accidents that people experience happen at home. We need to work to create safer living environments both inside and around our homes — whether this is the home you want to remain in or there will be other homes in the future.

This would be true for all homes that you might live in over your lifetime, whether you occupied them as a homeowner or a renter.

How Does Universal Design Relate To "ADA"?

The concepts of "ADA" or the "Americans With Disabilities Act" specify what must be addressed and in what manner to make indoor spaces and entrances (non-residential) accessible to everyone — especially people using a wheelchair or other forms of mobility assistance such as a cane or walker.

Generally, accessibility equates with safety because the openness or ease of approaching and using something promotes safe access.

While some people may think that universal design is akin to meeting ADA requirements, this is not true.

Universal design solutions, treatments, fixtures, components, features, strategies, and elements are complementary to that ideal in many ways.

They just aren't required or labeled as such for residences.

In some ways, ADA requirements hinder rather than promote safety, such as with the placement of grab bars and railings. Fortunately, the requirements do not apply in residential construction. Thus, you should use what makes sense from a safety or universal design standpoint in your home (or one you are working on) and leave the rest alone.

Single family homes, duplexes, triplexes, and quads are exempt from the provisions of ADA although some local building codes could require some compliance. Nevertheless, accessibility is a great idea. Let's just make sure that we are doing it safely as well — to accommodate the well-being of everyone.

Universal design and ADA are not the same thing; however, designing to comply with ADA requirements may make sense. Just be careful to evaluate each installation ahead of time for safety concerns.

Benefiting From Universal Design

Essentially everyone can benefit from universal design ideals, strategies, and solutions.

That's why it has the name universal attached to it. Also, as more people desire to remain in the homes they love, they can incorporate such design considerations into their remodeling or updating plans.

It doesn't matter how the work gets done — just that these suggestions and treatments get used to afford more comfort, accessibility, safety, and general enjoyment in our homes.

You might be contemplating doing the work yourself, or you might be discussing it with a professional that you will engage to do all or part of it.

You might also be such a professional that will be suggesting, designing, or doing all or part of the work for someone else — meaning that you are an occupational therapist, physical therapist, other type of health care professional, electrician, plumber, carpenter, real estate sales professional, home stager, electrical services contractor (ESC), durable medical equipment (DME) specialist, home inspector, architect, HVAC contractor, appliance or plumbing fixture retailer, tile setter, cement mason, flooring contractor, flatwork contractor, or structural engineer.

Because universal design is meant to accommodate the widest range of ages and abilities, it is not driven by someone's specific physical ability or medical condition.

Neither is it limited to just owner-occupied residences. Depending on the extent and complexity of the design changes desired, many of the strategies I present in this text are appropriate for renters and building owners as well.

Universal Design And Normal Aging

As a homeowner or renter, you are looking for solutions and concepts that will help you be more comfortable in your home now. You want to be able to use the fixtures and features that you have — or that you add or replace them with — safer and more conveniently.

You also want to be safe and comfortable in your home as the years go by — whether you are living by yourself or have others in your home with you.

Because people age in different ways — based on a number of genetic, lifestyle, and environmental factors — some have more health concerns and daily living issues than others. Of course, there often are quite a variety of ages, heights, and abilities in a home — even multiple generations — so determine what works for you and your household and design accordingly.

Some people as they age have relatively few health issues and function as they have throughout their lives. They might be a little older, but they still enjoy being able to bike, hike, ski, golf, play tennis, bowl, swim, and have an active lifestyle. They do things around their home and are up to tackling renovations.

Climbing stairs, opening doors, and accessing and using other aspects of their home aren't serious concerns or issues for them.

Some people have a few aches and pains that they live with that don't impede their daily schedule or activities that much. In a sense, they have learned to accommodate what ails them, and they manage.

Others (regardless of their present age) have aging issues such as osteoporosis, arthritis, bursitis, and other joint issues in their hands, feet, ankles, hips, elbows, spine, and shoulders. They may have stiffness in these areas from sports injuries or other causes.

They might have vision, hearing, cognitive, or mobility issues (how they get around and move about). Range-of-motion, reaching, standing, sitting, stepping up and down, holding and carrying objects, and other common tasks around the home may not be as easy as they used to be.

Regardless of what issues might be present, or might come along, universal design is a great strategy for helping anyone to live well in their home. It allows for more access, safety, convenience, comfort, use of your home, and general peace-of-mind than any other type of decorating or remodeling approach.

2

Universal Design Has Huge Benefits

The Strength Of Universal Design

Accepting the concept or premise that universal design really is for all ages and abilities, it sets the stage for an array of improvements in our homes that enhance safety, accessibility, comfort, convenience, security, and other important aspects.

Since universal design will accommodate the reach, hand and arm strength, range-of-motion, coordination, and physical abilities of a child (say a 4-, 5-, or 6-year old) as well as a 90-year old, and someone who is normally ambulatory to someone who typically uses a walker or wheelchair for assistance, it then becomes the preferred design strategy for helping anyone enjoy their home — regardless of the number of occupants.

Universal design allows accessibility and use of the various aspects of any home — inside and out— in a safe, friendly, comfortable, and convenient manner without any adaptation or other considerations.

However, these features and treatments also facilitate later adaptation for specific needs or for changes in someone's physical ability over time.

It doesn't matter whether someone is standing or seated, with their full range-of-motion or some limitations, having unrestricted mobility or some mobility issues, with no stamina or coordination issues or moderate ones, and even with moderate cognitive issues — universal design accommodates these varying abilities and uses.

The Safety Benefit Of Universal Design

Major reasons or benefits for wanting to have universal design strategies and solutions implemented in your home or for people you are working with (if you are a provider) include *safety, security, comfort, convenience, function* (usefulness), *accessibility, marketability* (resale value), *visitability, sustainability* (durable and cost-effective improvements), and *peace-of-mind.*

Any one of these reasons would be sufficient for creating universal design solutions and strategies for anyone, but most people will benefit from all of them.

Safety is the subject of this book and, as such, is a key objective in remodeling or renovating a home or apartment.

In general, universal design elements result in more safety because they provide more lighting, easier opening drawers and doors, more stable footing and standing surfaces (inside and outside), easier to use controls, better hygiene, other helpful solutions, and a more secure living environment.

They aren't dependent on someone's physical size or ability to use them correctly or effectively.

Universal design choices also provide convenience, comfort, and economic benefits (expressed in a variety of ways such as having more durable features and fixtures that won't need replacing), but mostly they make our living spaces safer.

This, in turn, promotes security, both within the four or more walls and around the property. Not worrying about falling, tripping, or stumbling on unsafe flooring or clutter, being confused by busy designs and furnishings, able to access controls and windows, relying on impact-resistant windows, and having proper lighting increases safety, comfort, peace-of-mind, and security.

Security is often represented by peace-of-mind.

More Universal Design Benefits

By making things in and around the home more accessible and easier to use, generally they also are more convenient to use and more enjoyable — regardless of how tall someone is, whether they are seated or standing, or what their range-of-motion, ability to reach or lift objects, or other limitations or concerns might be.

People can be more comfortable and confident with setting the temperature, using various fixtures and appliances, using water at a pleasant and safe temperature, accessing controls without having to reach for them or stretch to see what the settings are, and generally moving about in the home.

In terms of marketability, universal design changes and improvements can make any home easier to sell or rent later on because it will appeal to a broader section of the population and have more actual value or more perceived value — achieving a higher sales price or rent and fewer days on the market.

Think in terms of modernizing your home or living space to make it more attractive for you and your guests or visitors, making it more contemporary, using newer technology, and achieving more style — in addition to just making the changes because of the safety, convenience, or comfort benefits.

There is a real economic and aesthetic benefit to making universal design changes. Moreover, because they are intended to be unobtrusive and essentially invisible except as a design feature, these treatments have tremendous visual appeal and will be attractive additions to any home.

Benefits For Visitors

A big reason for incorporating universal design changes into anyone's home is for visitability — the ability of people coming to ours for any purpose to be able to access them and feel welcome.

Of course, personal safety and general enjoyment of your home still top the list for making improvements. This is an often overlooked reason for making home modification, however.

Whenever someone entertains or hosts a meeting, party, get-together, backyard party or cookout, dinner, reception, or discussion group — or if someone (a friend or not, expected or not) just drops by — they want people to feel welcome in coming to their home without wondering if their guests will feel comfortable and at-ease.

People hosting the event won't always know in advance whether someone can climb steps or negotiate a narrow entryway — when that is the case. Maybe someone they invited brings along a friend or relative of theirs who has mobility issues.

Therefore, we need to make our homes as "visitable" as possible — capable of being entered and navigated without restrictions, limitations, or worry by anyone we invite or who comes along with someone else who was invited.

Also, as we grow older, the chances increase that our friends and relatives will need some type of mobility assistance (cane, walker, or wheelchair), that they might have balance issues, or that they will have difficulty with hip or knee joints that hinder climbing steps. We may not think of this in advance.

By making visitable improvement to our homes to allow comfortable access to the main public areas of our homes (entry, foyer, hallway, living room, dining room, family room, bathroom, kitchen), this shows a thoughtfulness and anticipation on our part to accommodate our guests and relatives that they should notice and appreciate when they come for a visit.

In addition to providing access, visitability also creates a safer environment because our visitors and guests will be able to enter and traverse our homes without difficulty. They won't need to be concerned about any challenges they might face in climbing steps or getting through narrow doorways or hallways because we already will have thought about those issues and taken the necessary measures to correct them — visitable design and improvements.

Using Universal Design

To achieve greater safety inside and around our homes, to offer more comfort and convenience to us and the people who live in our home along with us (as well as those who visit on occasion), and to enhance the value and resale potential of our homes, there are many things that can be done — some as a do-it-yourself project for those who feel up to it, or by others we can engage to help us get the job done. The majority of these changes and treatments are going to universal design.

We'll start by looking at and discussing those features, concepts, treatments, and design elements that are relatively simple and inexpensive that often can be done without a building permit, inspection, or any demolition or construction. This means minimal dust and mess also — regardless of who does the work.

In fact, other than knowing that something has been added, moved, changed, or removed from what was there previously (or that a general room renovation has occurred), no one will ever know any work was done. This is the great thing about universal design improvements — they just fit in.

The next day, our homes will look like they always have been that way. Some items may be a little shinier or newer looking than the others, but that would likely be the only reason they would stand out.

So we'll start with those easy fixes that involve switches of various types and functions, drawer pulls, door knobs and locks, and lighting.

Then we'll move on from there to items that are going to require some construction (and possibly some demolition) and will be a little more disruptive or possibly create some minor inconvenience until they are completed.

Existing plumbing fixtures, major appliances, flooring, cabinetry, windows, wall mounted controls, electric outlets, towel bars, mirrors, and similar items will be addressed — along with things such as grab bars, other kitchen and bathroom features, auxiliary lighting, and items for the exterior of our homes.

All of these are going to be from a universal design approach that creates comfort, safety, accessibility, ease of use, and convenience for everyone in our homes — regardless of their physical size or ability.

3

Easy Universal Design Solutions

Starting With The Easy Fixes

There are several changes that can be made in our homes to make them more comfortable, safe, convenient, or accessible that require nothing more than taking out what is there and replacing it with a more suitable product or item — or simply removing it and doing without it. Essentially anyone can do it.

As a homeowner or renter, you or someone in your family can do it. A neighbor or friend can do it. A handyman can do it. A remodeler, contractor, or builder can do it.

These changes make a big and important) improvement in our homes, but they usually require no building permit or inspection. They just make our homes safer to live in because there is less risk of accidents.

A little care is required, but they are easy to accomplish — depending on who does them and the number of tasks undertaken at one time.

These modifications cover aspects of electrical, plumbing, lighting, doors, and cabinets.

Some other changes that I will suggest as we go along will require some light construction and may mean a little dust, localized mess, and temporary disruption in a particular room or area of the home.

You just need to make sure that whoever does the work in your home — if it's not you or someone you know and trust very well — that it is a properly authorized and licensed activity for the person performing the work and that they have all of their insurance policies in force (such as general liability and worker's compensation). Make them show you proof of insurance.

Lever Door Handles

When I think of universal design, lever door handles are one of the first items that comes to mind. You may already have them, but if you don't let's start your universal design makeover here.

These are the epitome of universal design. This concept provides safety, comfort, and convenience as well as aesthetic appeal.

The use of the lever style door handle on any hinged door that opens in or out – including storm doors, screen doors, entrance doors, patio doors, and interior doors, whether or not they have locks or dead bolts – allow anyone to use them successfully.

This includes young people who are so short as to be barely able reach the handles with outstretched fingers and those with weakened hand or arm strength or severe range-of-motion limitations who may have difficulty extending their hands or using their fingers to grasp things such as a traditional door knob.

What makes the lever handle such an ideal universal design element is the way it can be operated and the door released to open in several different ways.

It has a large tolerance for error and requires low physical effort to use – two important guidelines of universal design.

Unlike a traditional round door knob that needs to be grasped and then turned to unlatch it, the lever style doesn't need to be grabbed or turned with the entire hand. Therefore, it doesn't take any particular amount of strength to hold onto or turn it.

It can be used with the full hand to operate it (even with arthritis or a hand that has trouble making a fist because grasping and turning are not part of the way this handle is used), just a couple of fingers to push down on it, the side of the hand (open or in a fist) to push on it, the back of the hand or wrist to push down, the elbow or forearm to push down, the sides of both hands together to apply enough release pressure when your hands are messy or when you're holding something that you can't put down easily (or supporting yourself on a cane or walker), or even with a box or something else you might be holding to push down on the lever.

In addition to accommodating a wide range of ages and physical abilities, this door handle has the added practical benefit of being able to be operated when your hands are full with something you really don't want to set down or can't put down easily — or when your hands might be messy or greasy and you'd rather not grasp the lever and then have to go back later and clean it. Your hands might also be supporting you on a cane or walker.

From a safety standpoint, the levers can be operated successfully while wearing a heavy glove or mitten (if you've been doing outside work or it's cold outside) or while using a towel to prevent transfer of whatever you might have on your hands.

From an aesthetic standpoint, the lever handles provide a nice sleek, clean, modern, contemporary look and are available in several styles, finishes, and colors — with and without locks.

For those that want an immediate solution without replacing every door knob in the home, the rounded knobs can be fitted with a device — also available in various colors and finishes — that adapts the knobs to look and function like a lever handle.

Conversely, a lockset and door handle that is tricky to use and presents safety issues because it can cause discomfort while using it is the thumb-latch style entry lockset. This clearly is not a universal design. While they may be attractive because they remind us of an earlier time, they aren't practical or recommended.

It takes a lot of thumb pressure to release the latch and is often a two-handed operation — depressing the latch with one thumb or side of your hand and holding it that way while grasping the handle and pulling or pushing the door open with the other. There is not much tolerance for error in using this.

Even if you personally can operate it, think visitability and the abilities of others in your home.

Rocker Light Switches

I also think of the rocker or "Decora" brand light switches when I think of universal design. These and the lever style door handles top the list of universal design features for me. Literally, anyone who can reach or touch this style of light switch can use it.

Both the door handle and the light switch offer a component of safety, comfort, and convenience in being able to use them so flexibly.

Both require low physical effort and can accommodate a wide tolerance for error with almost no risk of hurting your hand or fingers.

You can push on the light switch in the middle or on any other part of it. It will turn on or off, as needed without pushing it "exactly right."

You can use one finger, the tip of a finger, the flat of your hand, a fist, the side of your hand, the back of your hand, your wrist, your elbow, your shoulder, or even an object that you might be holding in your hand — basically anything that provides enough contact and pressure to move the switch into the on or off position.

Again, if you are holding something, holding onto something, steadying or balancing yourself (with a cane or walker, for instance), or your hands are dirty and you don't want to make a mark on the switch, switchplate, or wall, the rocker or Decora switch is great.

Contrast this with the tiny toggle-style switch that typically must be grasped or pushed with more physical effort and with greater accuracy that the rocker switches — there is no comparison.

In terms of aesthetics, the rocker or Decora switches provide a clean, modern, contemporary look, while the toggle switches look a little old-fashioned.

The rocker switches are a great universal design solution, but in many ways they are just the accepted style to use. They definitely fit in and are probably more noticeable today when they aren't used than when they are.

You may already have them in your home (in some locations or everywhere). If you do, you now can appreciate the benefit of having and using them for the safety, comfort, and convenience they offer.

Illuminated Light Switches

A small but important modification for light switches (for the rocker or Decora style) is getting them with a small light in them that makes them easy to find in dim light, in darkened rooms, or at night.

They're great for your guests and visitors, too.

Simply take out the existing rocker switches and replace them with these or do this as you are replacing the old-style toggle switches.

This adds safety and convenience — plus the comfort of knowing that the light switch can be located.

Motion Sensor Light Switches

If you already have the rocker or Decora light switches, or you are swapping out toggle switches for rocker or Decora, here's a simple modification you can make. Install a motion sensor (also called motion detector or movement sensor) light switch that mounts in the same space as the switch it is replacing. This can provide peace-of-mind and added safety as well as convenience in low traffic areas.

The switch turns on any light that is controlled by it — ceiling fixture or switched lamp (plugged into a wall outlet controlled by that switch) with incandescent, florescent, LED, or halogen bulbs — and stays on for either a fixed period of time or for a time that can be set to turn off the lights after the sensor detects no movement in the room.

When you enter a darkened room — such as a powder room or guest bedroom — with something in your hands to put away in that room (paper goods, towels, linens, or clean laundry) you can take care of your mission without being concerned about locating or using the light switch — or about tripping over something that you didn't see in the dark. This works great for visitors and guests also.

If you are using a cane, walker, or wheelchair — or this applies to someone else in your home, or possibly a guest or visiting relative — this saves them moving to where the light switch is located and then actually using the light switch to illuminate the room. This gives them greater peace-of-mind and a safer environment.

This also provides a measure of security by having lights that come on as if someone in the home has turned them on — when someone or something not expected to be present is detected.

Even if you are home but are not in that part of your home where the motion is detected, this is a tremendous safety and security feature for you because it will look from the outside like you responded to the noise or activity.

For exterior lighting, fixtures are available that are solar powered and motion sensitive can be placed anywhere — on the fascia, on a pole, on a fence, on a porch railing or post, on the garage — without needing electric wiring to run them. This adds to your security, safety, and peace-of-mind.

Timer Light Switches

A similar idea for switching on and off lights at pre-determined times but with a little less flexibility than having a light come on due to motion when someone enters a room and turn off when they leave is to use an electric timer that plugs into an electrical outlet.

These are inexpensive switches that can be used anywhere in your home (even outdoors if they are rated for exterior use) where you want lights to come on regularly at the same time. They allow one or more lamps to plug into the timer and be turned on and off at fixed times that you determine and set.

You can change the activation times as daylight hours get longer or shorter, and there is an override switch when you want to turn the light on even when it is scheduled to be off. The timer works well for operating holiday, outdoor, or decorative lighting also.

Just be aware that when the power goes off, the timer will be affected so check it periodically to make sure it reflects the correct time — also adjust it an hour forward or back for the semi-annual time change.

Photo Cell Light Switches

This is another alternative that you can use for exterior lighting and indoor lamps (for safety, security, comfort, and convenience) when they only need to be on at night. Instead of relying on a manual switch or an electric timer, a photo cell can be used to turn the lights on when you need them at night.

It can be part of the light fixture or a separate sensor switch that is screwed into the light socket with the bulb then screwed into it.

The sensor will turn the lights on that it controls when the ambient lighting has dropped to a low enough level to require the lights to come on. They will turn off again when there is sufficient daylight to switch them off. They do wear out occasionally and need to be replaced, but they do not require any other maintenance.

This can take care of lighting important areas of your home — inside and outside — without you remembering to do it or when it might already be dark when you come home. This definitely enhances safety by being able to light your way in the areas you have selected.

Sometimes they'll come on and remain on when the sky is very cloudy or during a heavy rain or snowfall, and nearby lights might interfere with their sensory ability — causing them to flicker or shut off prematurely.

Programmable/Preset Light Switches

This is another safety, convenience, and efficiency option available for you to include in your home.

In addition to other methods for controlling when your lights operate, a device that will fit into a standard switch box can be used to have lights come on and stay on for a fixed period of time before turning off — either preprogrammed or set by you. The lights aren't affected by movement.

Digital Thermostats

This solution allows anyone in the home to access and use the device in a comfortable, convenient, and safe way. That's what makes it universal.

It's just means taking out a manual, dial–type or slide–switch style mercury thermostat and replacing it with one that has a digital display — programmable or not.

Some digital thermostats have the ability to be set and control temperatures for various times of the day or for multiple days. Some just maintain the temperature as it is set — for heating or cooling — until changed.

Either way, they can be read from a few feet away and don't rely on grasping a dial or switch and trying to move it a small amount. Some can even be controlled remotely from smartphones and tablets.

Obviously, this is good for all ages and even people with some vision or coordination difficulties. This is what makes it easier and safer to use — and to take the guesswork out of what the setting or the present temperature is.

The thermostat is easily changed out by you as the homeowner or renter (or a friend, neighbor, or relative), but it also can be done by a handyman or remodeler as part of a larger project.

It can be replaced exactly where is has been, but an even better strategy is to move it to a lower position so it is more accessible and visible to everyone.

This will require a little more work to move the wiring so the first step would be just to replace the old thermostat with a digital one. Then it can be lowered later to a more accessible and convenient position.

Door/Drawer Pulls

Opening doors and drawers in the kitchen, bathrooms, laundry room, and elsewhere throughout the house can present issues for people with small hands, weak hand or arm strength, or arthritis in their hands or fingers. This also applies to dressers, night stands, end tables, armoires, and other furniture with drawers or doors.

In order to make it easier for everyone to access and use them safely, this one universal design change of replacing those knobs and pulls with ones easier to use can make a huge difference and really dress up the appearance of a kitchen or bath (or furniture) and give it a modern look at the same time.

Depending on which hardware is selected and the number of cabinet drawers and doors in the kitchen, bathrooms, laundry room, garage, basement, and elsewhere in the home, it may not be an inexpensive change but one that is easily done. It can even be done a little at a time if this is something you are going to be doing yourself.

What you want to achieve are door and drawer handles and pulls that require little-to-no gripping strength to operate — unlike that needed for using small knobs that have to be grasped before they can be leveraged to open the door or drawer.

You are going for ease of use and safety, and you want plenty of room to insert your fingers into the pull rather than just your fingertips so you reduce the risk of your hand slipping off and assuring that you actually can open the door or drawer.

Some people even like the idea of using a folded leather strap attached to the door as a pull on a pantry or other large door that can be grabbed or used by inserting your hand into it.

Whatever approach you decide to take, your existing door and drawer pulls can easily be switched out by removing them and attaching the new ones with the same mounting holes — as long as you select new ones that have the two mounting posts 3" apart (or whatever spacing is present) like the ones you are replacing.

Pulls that require wider or narrower mounting holes than what exists will require drilling new holes and possibly patching and touching up the existing ones.

For the knobs that have just a single mounting bolt, a second hole (or sometimes two holes to achieve a center alignment) will need to be drilled.

This is easily done by creating a template out of paper, cardboard, or thin wood to get all of the holes in the same place on the various doors and drawer fronts. Just align it in the same place on every door or drawer.

Again, some patching and touchup might be required for the unused former holes.

A major safety concern to be aware of for existing and new pulls is that any material on the pull surface that sticks out past the main part of the pull can catch clothing or skin when someone walks by too closely or comes in contact with it.

As an alternate to using door pulls, some people like to use magnetic latches that hold a door closed until the lock is released by depressing it slightly with the door front and allowing it to "pop" open.

This eliminates any issues that someone might have with hand or arm strength or range-of-motion in pulling open a cabinet door. Just a pushing motion on the door will release the latch and allow the door to open.

Additionally, some doors also will remain closed with tension or spring assisted hinges or just the weight of the door without using a catch to secure it — and open by grasping a corner or edge of the door and gently pulling on it.

Such doors typically do not have a door pull and provide a cleaner, more uniform look that way.

The issue with doors that have no pulls on them — or that don't use pulls to release the latch and open the doors — is that they aren't as intuitive to use and may be confusing for guests or visitors.

Still, they are common enough in usage that someone likely has seen them elsewhere and generally can figure out how to use them.

Single-Lever Faucets

When I think of universal design, another one of the first items that comes to mind is the single-lever faucet — for safety, comfort, accessibility, and convenience.

This is a classic example of universal design and one that is extremely functional as well as modern looking and visually appealing.

It truly works for all ages and abilities — especially anyone who might have issues with hand or arm strength, stamina, dexterity, coordination, balance, reach, range-of-motion, or insensitivity to feeling heat in their hands.

It's already included in many homes just because of its appearance, but if you don't already have this you can easily swap out any existing dual-style or two-handle faucet set with the single-lever model if you have the tools and experience to do light plumbing work. If not, it's an easy project for a friend or relative to tackle.

The important thing to remember is to remove all the residue and gaskets or putty from the existing installation so the new one can be installed on a clean, dry surface — using new gaskets and putty as recommended or included with the new faucet.

Of course, handymen, remodelers, or plumbers can do this as part of a larger project. Just make sure the replacement faucet uses the same holes that are already present in the sink or countertop or that it completely covers and seals any of the unused ones. Don't leave any holes exposed.

While the single-lever faucet is more stylish and contemporary than two-handle faucets, style or price is not the main concerns. It's function. Aside from offering a sleek, modern look, the single-lever faucet offers significant safety benefits over the two-handle style.

The single-lever faucet can be operated by anyone who can reach it — without being overly concerned about someone accidently burning or hurting themselves by dispensing hot water unexpectedly.

The faucet handle and mixer would have to be positioned all the way to the far left and have the hot water come on rather instantly for this to be a concern.

Contrast that with someone using a sink with two faucet handles and not paying attention or understanding that the left side is the hot water control and being indifferent to the water temperature as long as they were able to have water coming out — until it may be too late to avoid discomfort or a mild burn.

Another safety benefit that the single-lever faucet affords that likely everyone can appreciate and relate to is being able to use it while you are preparing food.

After handling raw meat, eggs, or fish, or having sauces or something sticky, dirty, greasy, or messy on your hands, you can turn on the faucet and have the water come on without touching the handle directly with your affected hands (and transferring whatever is on your hands to the faucet handle). In fact, there are several ways of activating the lever without actually grabbing, holding, or specifically touching it in the normal manner.

Depending on the type and size of the lever, you can turn on the faucet with your forearm, fist, wrist, back of your hands, heel of your hands, elbows, while wearing kitchen gloves or using a towel you are holding to avoid direct contact, a wooden spoon or other kitchen utensil, or even a bowl or pot you might be holding.

This flexibility in use and low physical effort are hallmarks of universal design.

There also are faucets available now that just require some type of light contact along the spout to activate the water flow (and turn it off again) — less intuitive for a guest or visitor but very convenient for those accustomed to using it. However the valve does need to remain on and the temperature setting pre-selected for this to work effectively.

Generally, the water temperature is more consistent with a single-lever faucet than the two-handle system when the water is turned off and then back on again because the temperature mixing does not have to be redone.

Although the water is subject to cooling off — depending on the length of time that has passed since the single-lever faucet was last used (and the distance from the hot water heater to the faucet) — the water is relatively the same temperature as it was when it was turned off (or it soon will be as soon as the hot water flows back to it).

With a two-handle faucet system, the water has to be remixed by turning on each handle and then testing the water temperature until it feels about the way it was previously — unless it had been turned on with only cold or only hot water.

To make sure that you or someone else in your home doesn't accidentally turn on the hot water when you or they didn't intend to or expect it, a universal design gadget that you may want to get or request — for those spouts that will accept them — is a screw-on adapter in the place of a typical aerator that provides a blue light (for cold water) or red light (for hot water) to the water stream to indicate its relative temperature.

This non-electric light doesn't present any type of shock concern (it is battery operated and is reflected into the water stream to create the illusion of colored water), and it is an immediate visual clue for the general water temperature as well as great fun for kids and a conversation starter when guests are present.

Another option is selecting a faucet that already has a built-in light to indicate the relative temperature. There are several that do this.

Single-lever faucets should be used throughout the home — kitchens (including islands), baths (including powder rooms), laundry rooms, mud rooms, garages, summer kitchens, wet bars, patios, and basements.

Another safety, comfort, and convenience issue to remember involves the choice of the faucet spout to provide enough room to get your hands (or a dish, plate, glass, or pot) under the flowing water stream without contacting the back of the sink.

Also watch for splashing and spray from a spout that is designed too tall or high (resulting in a lot of splash or water bounce off the bottom of the sink to the surrounding countertop, floor, or whoever is using the sink).

Also, some faucets are angled or contoured to the point that water tends to hit the bottom of the sink and refract directly out onto the person using it. Shallow bowls and vessel sinks (because of their shape) tend to create more splash issues than others and impact the safety, comfort, and convenience of those using them.

Convenience Water Faucets

There are two other types of faucets that often are found at the sink that can present safety issues. In general, they are installed for comfort and convenience, but this can backfire without exercising due caution.

The first is found in the kitchen at the main sink although it could be found at an island sink, wet bar sink, or outdoor sink. This is an instant hot water dispenser used for making hot tea, instant coffee, hot chocolate, or an instant cup of soup. It can be used for dissolving gelatin or for cooking when very hot water is needed.

It is activated by a single lever (turned, lifted, or depressed by pushing down on it), but there is no temperature adjustment at the point of delivery. This needs to be adjusted under the sink. As such, the water is delivered — steaming hot — when the faucet is opened.

By design, it is universal because everyone who is tall enough to reach it and access it can turn it on and use it; however, the issue is one of safety.

While it provides a measure of convenience (instead of waiting while water heats on the cooktop or stove, or in the microwave), if the water is hot enough to do what it is intended to do (up to 200 degrees), it can mildly injure someone who accidentally places their hand under the stream, has the very hot water splash on their skin, or is taken off-guard when the heat transfer through the cup or vessel is more than expected.

The safety concerns may not outweigh the convenience benefits, but extreme care needs to be exercised in installing and using this feature.

Setting the temperature on the unit lower might help reduce the burning risk, but it might have to be set too low for the hot water to be useful. Determine the benefits of having this installed in your home before going forward with it.

The second type of convenience faucet is a spout or spigot at the sink just for filling a drinking glass or drinking from it directly.

This is universal in design and application as long as everyone in your home can activate the faucet lever.

The only concern is water that might splash from the faucet onto the person using the water tap — or onto the countertop or floor. This could create a minor inconvenience and possibly a slipping hazard until the errant water was cleaned up.

Pot-Fillers

Another type of single lever faucet that is often used in the kitchen is the pot filler. This is found in new construction and in recently remodeled homes. However, these are not universal design features and have many safety issues associated with them.

Typically pot fillers are located in the backsplash above the stove or cooktop — although I have seen them on an island, at an auxiliary sink, or at the main sink.

A pot filler certainly supplies convenience — being able to fill a stockpot, double boiler, saucepan, or any other cooking vessel right from the cooking surface without having to carry it to the stove or cooktop from the sink.

What happens that makes it unsafe and keeps it from being a universal design strategy is that it gives people a false sense of well-being. They are struck by the convenience of filling their cooking vessel right at the stove or cooktop and don't relate the weight of the water (8 pounds per gallon or roughly 25 pounds for a 3 gallon container) to what they are doing — or in what it will take to dispose of the water once the cooking is finished.

Since they are not filling the pot or pan at the sink and then walking with it over to the stove or cooktop (whatever the distance is), they are disconnected from the process and have no idea how much it might weigh or if they can pick it up or move it again after they are done using it — even if only some of the liquid remains.

People risk spilling or splashing the liquid in the pot or pan on themselves or the floor, knocking over or dropping the pot, or hurting themselves as they strain to lift something relatively heavy at an awkward height (perhaps even shoulder height). They may find that they will need to bail the liquid into smaller containers before being able to lift the pot.

There are the additional safety issues of needing to reach (possibly over a hot or warm burner that may be in use) to access the pot filler, and having a water source over the stove that could drip if not shut off properly or splash if turned on too much while filling.

When young people want to help out in the kitchen, they are not going to be able to access the pot filler or move the heavy pot unless they are tall teen-agers.

While this fixture is modern and attractive, the safety and accessibility issues concerned with using it outweigh its usefulness.

Pipe Wrapping

One more issue concerning the plumbing in your home that you can handle easily — or have it done easily — is wrapping the exposed water pipes and traps under the sinks if people are likely to come in contact with them.

If they are contained inside a cabinet or vanity, it's not really a concern. This is only a potential safety issue for members of your household and for guests if they might bump into them.

It's not so much that people can injure or burn themselves from direct contact with the hot water pipes in your home. They can, but the hot water is not present in the pipes at temperature except when the faucet is open and hot water is being delivered at a particular fixture.

Interior Painting

In most cases, painting walls, trim, and ceilings (or staining furniture or molding) is something that you as the homeowner or renter can accomplish — depending on how big the job is, how high the ceilings are, and your balance, coordination, stamina, range-of-motion, and ability to use your arms to reach above you or your legs to climb and stand on ladders.

You can certainly hire a professional painter, handyman, decorator, or remodeler if you don't feel up to tackling the task or want it done quickly with no mess or cleanup to worry about.

There are three issues to consider about painting.

First, if you are concerned about indoor air quality or that characteristic paint smell that goes along with such a project, look for and select low- or no-VOC paint (volatile organic compounds). They are more money than paint that contains higher amounts of VOC, but it will eliminate the strong vapors that often go along with painting. Finding low-VOC paint is not difficult.

Second, if you have a popcorn ceiling as a surface finish anywhere in your home, it may have asbestos in it. As long as you don't disturb it, you are fine. As you go to paint it, you could loosen some of it. Have your ceiling checked before beginning if you are unsure as to whether it contains asbestos and if it might be an air quality issue for you.

Third, if your home was built in 1977 or earlier, it falls under the Lead Paint Rule of the EPA. You should engage a professional to test your air quality for lead particles before painting or remodeling just to be safe.

Keypad Entry Door Locks

This is a practical solution that affords additional safety, security, convenience, and peace-of-mind.

Replace existing entry door locksets with a push button or keypad lock system, and make sure to get a lockset with a lever handle.

Simply take out your existing front door lockset and replace it with the keypad one. There are different colors and finishes available.

This design works for all ages, but get a keypad with the largest numbers possible to make it easier to read and to be able to touch the keys without difficulty.

If you have young children or grandchildren who can be trusted with the combination, they can unlock the door by pressing the correct numbers or letters. There is no worry of them losing a key or for you trying to keep track of how many people have been issued keys.

Everyone in your household (or those to whom you grant access) can unlock the door by just punching in the correct combination of letters, numbers, or pattern, and the lock can be reprogrammed as often as desired for additional security. This is also great for your extended family (or trusted neighbors) that may visit regularly but not live at your address.

For additional safety and security, your keypad lock can be programmed with a separate combination for temporary access each time repair and service technicians or personnel need to enter your home — so that the actual combination is not handed out or revealed and there is no need to have a key given to them or hidden outside for them.

Of course, you can reprogram the lock as often as you feel comfortable in doing so. Just make sure to let everyone who needs access to your home what the new combination is (and be sure to write it down where you can find it again later).

4

More Extensive And Intensive Universal Design Solutions

Going Beyond The Easy Fixes

We just looked several improvements, changes, treatments, and modifications you can do to make your home safer that require hardly any work other than swapping out less efficient or effective light switches, door handles, cabinet and drawer handles and pulls, and faucets.

Now, we want to consider many other changes that can make your home more comfortable, safe, convenient, or accessible that require some advance planning and some professional help.

Unless you are very skilled in doing some of this work yourself as a homeowner, you are going to require the help of contractors and other professionals to help you accomplish the design strategies and solutions that I discuss in this chapter.

Some construction and demolition (and dust) will likely be required to complete these changes. That's why it may take the work of professionals to accomplish it.

Depending on which of these changes you undertake, and the extent of them, they might be able to be accomplished without a building permit or inspection.

These changes are meant to be as invisible as possible, but you will appreciate the improvements that they will make to your home. They just may not stand out as being something special or different.

Using Open Doorways

For a great universal design solution that is aesthetic, sustainable, and practical, create the illusion of a doorway for dividing space or separating rooms.

These open doorways maximizes accessibility, visitability, and safety because they can be nearly as wide as the hallway or space they are framing by creating the illusion of a doorway without presenting a narrow opening to negotiate or a physical door to operate.

On long entry halls that take people from the front of your home to the back, such a feature (sometime with a glass or decorative transom over it) can be used to define the separation of the front of the house from the back, but no door needs to be mounted because there is no need to close off the space.

Archway passages as entrances to a master suite vestibule or a secondary bedroom wing function the same way. They act as a doorway but remain open at all times because there is no door attached to them. The doorway is implied rather than actually created.

In the same way, they can also be used as entrances for dining rooms or family rooms or other areas in your home to indicate where the spaces begin but are totally open and accessible.

36" Doorways

This is another one of the items that tops my list of universal design features. It is such an intuitive an practical solution, but it has yet to be embraced by the majority of the nation's homebuilders. As such, most homes do not have them.

If more homes came with 36" doorways (the size of the actual door itself rather than the finished opening which generally is somewhat smaller) already included, homeowners would not have to incur the time, expense, and inconvenience (regardless of who does the work) of replacing the existing doors with larger ones.

Unless 36" interior doorways (or "3-0" as they are called in construction) are specifically requested, most new homes are designed with 32" (called "2-8" in construction terminology) or smaller doorways.

The difference in wall and floor space between a 32" and 36" doorway is 4", but that is a very important 4" for universal design, accessibility, and safety.

There is a very practical reason as well for all interior doorways to be 36" wide — many exterior doorways already are 36" (or larger when double doors are used). Anyone who has ever moved a mattress or bed frame into a bedroom — or other furniture from room-to-room in a home or apartment — knows how challenging it can be dealing with a 32" or smaller doorway compared to one that is 36".

Skinned knuckles, bruised shins, and dinged furniture — or even getting furniture stuck or wedged into the doorway opening — have resulted from narrow doorways.

It's sometimes hard enough to deal with a 36" doorway, but that is so much better than smaller ones. Anything larger than 36" such as 40" (while being helpful) would be noticeable and contrary to our universal design objective of creating invisible and unobtrusive solutions, treatments, and improvements.

Nevertheless, just giving everyone a safer and easier time of moving furniture or other items about between rooms in the home or apartment is reason enough for having the wider 36" doorways.

The visitability factor comes into play when we note that a wheelchair may need 29" or more of clearance — with a 32" width being the published design guideline — just to negotiate safely through a doorway.

While a 32" doorway is wide enough in theory to accommodate wheelchair access for someone living in your home (or an occasional visitor), it doesn't measure up. Taking into account a door thickness of 1⅜" or more (1¾" for a solid core door), a hinge of another ¾" or so, and the stop (nearly another ⅜"), the effective clearance in a 32" doorway has been reduced by some 2½" or more.

In order to achieve a true 32" or larger effective passageway for easy wheelchair access in a home, 36" doors are the minimum size that should be used. A few inches wider would be even better, but 36" doorways are currently the widest size commonly available.

In some cases, pocket doors — mounted inside the walls — or sliding doors (also called "barn doors") — hung along the inside or outside walls of the doorway — may provide a wider effective opening as well.

Mounting pocket doors inside the walls will require some demolition and construction — and possibly moving some electric wiring and light switches, but surface mounted doors do not require any major construction as long as they don't cover a light switch or wall outlet — just installing the track and hanging the door along with removing the stop, striker plate, hinges, and casing from the door jamb and then patching as required to leave a smooth opening.

Either one of these solutions may be a larger job than you are willing to tackle on your own, and a handyman or remodeler can be used.

To swap out the 32" or smaller door with the 36" door, it's often just a matter of removing the existing doorway (door, jamb, and molding), enlarging the opening, and then replacing it with the larger 36" door — making sure it is plumb and square so it opens freely.

To complete this project, the drywall will to be trimmed, patched, and painted, and the doorway opening may need to be reframed. Wiring and light switches may have to be moved as well.

This can be a do-it-yourself project but you might want the help of a handyman, carpenter, or remodeling contractor — especially for doorways at the end of hallways that cannot be enlarged without first making the hallways wider. To widen the hallways, the space will need to be taken from the rooms bordering the hallway.

Widening Hallways

Even if you don't require a wider hallway to accommodate a doorway at the end of it, just having wider hallways goes along with concept of 36" doorways to make access in your home easier and therefore safer. However, it generally takes a lot more planning and work to accomplish.

This is not a matter of just removing a door and making the opening larger. This requires moving walls on either side of the hallway — at least one and likely two or more — depending on how it's configured.

To make hallways wider than the 36" or so that many typically are, the rooms with a common wall with the hallway will necessarily be affected as space for the wider hallway will be taken from them.

Widening hallways requires tearing out existing walls and reconstructing them a few inches away from where they were and toward the adjacent space. Some wiring and possibly air conditioning or heating ductwork will have to be relocated also.

The ceiling and flooring in the hallway will need to be redone or repaired as the space is widened into the original wall area where no ceiling or floor treatment existed (the walls were there and the current surfaces will be in their untreated, original state).

Hallways that are 42-45" in width seem to be field-tested and reasonable. Adding wall blocking as an adaptable design feature inside the hallway walls as they are rebuilt will facilitate installation of grab bars or other devices and fixtures at a later date as a needs-specific solution.

This project will likely require the services of a handyman, remodeler, HVAC contractor, electrician, painter, flooring contractor, and air quality inspector — and a dumpster or some other way of removing the construction debris.

Adjusting Door Swing

Occasionally, interior or exterior doors are mounted so that they open from the wrong side of the doorway opening or in the wrong direction (the way they swing open from their closed position) for the convenience, safety, and accessibility of those living in your home.

This means that the hinges need to be switched left-for-right or right-for-left to allow the door to open more desirably and conveniently for you.

The amount of room near the latch or door handle side of the door and the room to approach it and open it easily also factor into deciding whether the door swing should be adjusted. Use whatever is comfortable for you and anyone else in your home but generally figure on up to 24" of clear space to allow someone using mobility assistance to access the door handle easily.

In terms of safety, it could also be a matter of what the door opens into or onto — an adjacent wall, cabinets, fixtures, or furniture. Again, work to keep the approach zone by the door clear.

Reversing the swing from side to side, so that it opens opposite of where it is now but still in or out the same, requires a little work in terms of reversing the position of the hinges and striker plate and recess — plus patching, sanding, and painting where the hardware was before being moved.

Reversing whether the door opens in or out (except where local building codes require certain doors to open a particular way) requires a little more work. The stop and lockset have to be reversed also.

Unless you are particularly handy with woodworking, this is likely a job for a handyman, carpenter, or a remodeling contractor. Switching out the some of the targeted doors with pocket doors or sliding doors is also a possibility — depending on floor and wall space.

Closet Doors

Of course, there are many different styles of closet doors, depending on what room the closet is located in and what the purpose of the closet is.

There are bedroom closets — both wall closets with bypass, hinged, or bi-fold doors (or maybe even an old-style accordion door with pleats in it that slides along a track) as well as walk-in closets with pocket, bi-fold, or hinged doors.

Also, there are linen, coat, and utility closets in the hallway or foyer, and there are linen closets in or near the bath. There is the pantry and possibly laundry closet space in the kitchen (sometimes the hallway).

The same comments about door swing apply to closets in terms of accessibility and ease of use. Make sure there is a clear approach zone by the side or sides of the closet where the door handle is located.

If there is a hinged door, it might open into the closet, or it could open out into the hallway or into the room in which it is located. Bi-fold doors will stack to the side of the opening and protrude into the room — narrowing the walking space around them.

Bi-fold doors can severely restrict the passageway around them when they are located in a hallway, so the hallway needs to be wide enough to accommodate an opened bi-fold door and still allow someone to walk past it in the remaining space behind it without running into the opened door or the person accessing the closet. The same issue is present with a solid hinged door that opens out into the hallway.

Also, louvered bi-fold doors (the ones with slats in one or both halves of the door for ventilation and air flow) tend to attract dust and may present an indoor air quality or allergen issue for people susceptible to dust.

Because the closet door (hinged or bi-fold) must remain open while the closet is in use rather than just being opened to pass through it like door into a room (or kept closed for privacy), take a hard look at how each door is used before deciding if they need to be changed or allowed to remain as they are.

See if there are any potential obstructions preventing the door from opening fully or allowing others in your home to walk past it while it is open — assess how easy it is to operate the door and for the door to open easily to gain access to the closet.

For in-line pantry, supply, broom, linen closets and other such tall vertical compartments that are part of the cabinetry, dividing the space into smaller sections with smaller doors is better so that the doors aren't so heavy. This way, just one area of the closet or pantry can be accessed as needed rather than opening and handling a large door to open the entire space.

If you still have any of the accordion-style vinyl or fabric doors that slide along a track and collapse to one side as they are opened, you will want to replace them with a bi-fold, bypass, or sliding door. These doors tend to bind in the track as they are being opened or closed, and it often requires two hands to operate them effectively.

Bypass doors can be used when space is a concern and opening a door into a space may not be desirable. The concerns with bypass doors are that they restrict or limit access to just half of the closet at a time and they have a track on the floor in which the doors travel that could cause someone to catch their foot, walker, or wheelchair on it.

Again, if you are particularly handy with woodworking you can accomplished some of this, but this is likely a job for professionals such as a handyman, kitchen and bath designer, or a remodeling contractor.

Using Trench/Forward/Linear Drains

In a traditional bathtub — with or without a fixed shower head installation or a handheld shower that is used in addition to or in place of the shower head — the drain is located forward at the end of the tub.

However, in a stall shower — either manufactured or constructed on site — the drain in the shower pan is located in or near the middle.

The floor of the shower is formed into an inverse pyramid with the drain at the center. Even when the floor of the shower is formed without using a manufactured pan, it is still constructed with the same design and shape. To me, this is the wrong drain location for safety and comfort reasons.

First, the function of a shower is to get clean by washing away dirt with soap and water. Do you really want to stand in used soapy water while it drains — sometimes quite slowly and hindered because you are standing on the drain?

Your feet and ankles never get totally clean until you move away from the drain and rinse them again after most of the water completely drains — at the risk of slipping because you are walking in soapy water. Depending on how well and quickly the drain works, there can be a small pool of water around the drain.

Second, there is an uneven footing situation because of the way the floor slopes and pitches to the drain — from four different planes. This can be a slipping and balance issue, and many times, you will actually be standing right on the drain which is not particularly comfortable and it can interfere with the function of the drain.

Third, you often have to move about to try to get away from the water that is pooling at the drain, and this can result in slippery footing and potentially a dangerous fall.

Finally, if you want to stand on something such as a shower mat, a teak platform, or nonslip treads, these do not conform well to the inverse pyramid design and must be adapted to use them somewhat effectively and keep them from covering or blocking the drain.

The solution to this safety and comfort issue is to move the drain from the middle of the shower and put it back in the front like it is in the standard tub.

For homes built on a crawl space or basement, moving the drain a couple of feet is not a huge issue but will likely take professionals to do it. A slab foundation takes more work and more expense to break up part of the concrete and move the drain (drains for multiple shower locations), but is worth it for the safety and comfort achieved. Of course the flooring will need to be repaired or replaced.

The drain is the main issue. The faucet, mixer, and shower head may be fine where they are.

To allow water to drain faster and provide a sleeker look to the shower, a trench or linear drain is recommended. The plumbing below the drain remains the same with just the way the water is collected on the surface changing.

There are even surface drains that look much like the flush deco-drains used on pool decks that come in a variety of finishes, colors, styles, and patterns. Just be sure to choose a design that will provide safe footing and not allow anyone's foot or shower shoes to catch in any part of them.

The trench or linear drain that is located at the end of the shower ("forward"), with a flat shower floor gently pitched toward the drain, offers efficient draining and greater footing stability. Also, it accommodates the use of chairs, folding seats, or transfer benches in the shower as well as nonslip floor treatments.

Additionally, if someone else needs to be in the shower with you or someone else in your household to offer bathing assistance, it is easier for them to stand and move about on a flat service and one without the water pooling in the center.

It will take a little demolition and the work of a cement mason, a tile setter, a plumber, a handyman, kitchen and bath designer, or a remodeler to accomplish this drain makeover unless you are very skilled and confident in tackling a job such as this, but your family, overnight guests and the next owners of your home will thank you.

Zero-Step/No-Threshold/Barrier-Free Showers

When there is just a shower present in a bathroom with no bathtub, a big safety improvement is to remove the lip, threshold, transition, or step-up at the shower entrance to allow level access between the bathroom floor and the shower floor. This allows free access to the shower by anyone, regardless of their age or ability.

It may look a little different than traditional showers that have a lip, step up, or raised shower pan, but this "zero-step" shower entrance is becoming more popular and eliminates many of the safety and access concerns normally present.

As challenging as it might be to step into the shower (depending on the height of the step and the ability of the person using the shower), exiting the shower and stepping down to the bathroom floor presents a safety concern because your foot likely is wet from the shower (even if you have mostly dried yourself in the shower) and you are placing it on a potentially slippery tile surface. A bath mat can still slip as you step on it.

This project can be done at the same time as the floor drain relocation and shower floor modification. It will take a little demolition and the work of a cement mason, a tile setter, a plumber, a handyman, or a remodeler to accomplish unless you are very skilled at tackling a job such as this in your own home.

Shower Glass Enclosures/Shower Doors

To keep as much water inside the tub or shower as possible while taking a shower or using the handheld shower, many people have shower doors or other glass panels installed. The glass is generally tempered (which crumbles into tiny pieces when it is shattered), and sometimes plexiglas is used instead of glass (which can be just as jagged and sharp as glass when it is broken).

Generally, a single hinged door is used for a walk-in or stall shower, and a two- or three-panel bypass set of doors is used for a tub.

The sliding bypass tub doors are mounted in a track that covers the bath opening, and they slide inside and along a top and bottom track to keep water from splashing outside the tub or shower and onto the bathroom floor.

The lower track is held in place with adhesive caulk and the weight of the two or three doors on top of it. The side tracks are fastened to the walls or sides of the bath/shower area with screws or wall fasteners. The top track simply rests in place atop the two sides and has the weight of the doors (rolling along a track inside it) keeping it in place.

Just adding the extra height and width of the lower track is enough to create a potential tripping hazard or entrance barrier for those people with balance or coordination issues, those with relatively short legs, and those with range-of-motion issues in the hips, ankles, or knees.

One-piece shower doors for stall showers typically open out into the room and generally have magnetic or ball closures that open rather easily and allow most anyone to use them.

However, they can easily release and pop open when fallen against or used for support during a slip — increasing the likelihood of a more serious fall and injury.

If they have a locking mechanism strong enough to prevent opening with incidental or light contact, they can create a safety hazard of a different nature and not be suitable for use by those not strong enough to operate the door.

They also can impact the area of approach and clearance around the shower as sufficient space needs to be allowed for people to open the door freely — and for the doors left or moved into in the open position not to obstruct access to anything else in the bathroom.

Regular cleaning and maintenance of the glass or plexiglas panels to keep soap scum and mildew from forming or building up on the surface is important from a cleanliness and appearance standpoint. However, it can also be a safety issue in the shower space.

When the bypass doors — and even the clear glass panels that are often used as walls or dividers along with shower doors to define the wet space and prevent water from getting into the rest of the room when the shower is used — have soap or other build-up on their surfaces, they can become slippery.

Then, when the slippery surfaces are touched or leaned against (especially when they are wet or you are wet) — from incidental contact to being used to try to keep from falling after a slip or loss of balance — they will hasten rather than hinder a more serious fall.

Depending on how they are installed and the type of glass or plexiglas used, the panels may not be able to support someone's weight or withstand a fall into it in a panic situation such as loss of balance, a slip, or fall.

If these glass panels were to break, flex, or dislodge from their mounts or supports, a more serious accident than just a fall could result. Even a serious cut could happen.

Additionally, the glass doors and glass panels can reflect and refract light in a way that creates glare and affects orientation, depth perception, or the ability to tell where objects are located.

Glare can obscure some objects (potentially causing injury by walking into something that isn't clearly visible), and it can cause some surfaces to appear wet even when they aren't. Glare is a real safety concern.

Many of the shower door or shower area panels also have towel bars attached or bolted onto or through holes drilled in them, which — in a panic situation — are used as grab bars and may break, pull loose, or cause the doors or panels to come out of their tracks or otherwise fail to offer the support required.

In general, there are so many reasons of a safety, convenience, comfort, and accessibility nature for not using glass or plexiglas around a shower or bath area and not that many good ones that support their use.

It will take a little demolition and the work of a handyman, kitchen and bath designer, or a remodeler to remove the existing glass doors and panels (if you have them) unless you are a very skilled homeowner in tackling a job such as this. Removing the glass panels or doors will be awkward, and they may be heavy. They could have sharp edges. Also, they will need to be disposed of in some way.

Wet Room/Shower Room

For older homes with a relatively small hall bathroom (often the only bathroom in the home), creating a zero-step shower entrance presents additional challenges for keeping the rest of the room from getting wet when the shower is used.

One solution for this is to make the whole bathroom a wet room or shower room so that the entire space is capable of being wet.

It doesn't mean that you necessarily need to get everything in the bathroom soaked each time you take a shower. It just means that everything could get wet with no adverse effect — by intentional design.

Such a design further eliminates the need to consider keeping or adding glass partitions, shower doors, and even shower curtains.

It also allows the wet area of the shower (with one or more fixed showerheads or a handheld/personal shower) to be as large as necessary in the room without specifically defined boundaries.

This also facilitates using it effectively if you need to shower from a seated position on a bench or wheelchair, or if someone needs to assist you. It really adds flexibility to the bathroom.

Because all of the walls and floor are tiled, any water from the shower will drain to the primary or central floor drain, which can be located under the showerhead or linearly from wall-to-wall (and parallel to the room's entrance door) along the general edge of the shower area.

The floor would need to be pitched correctly for proper drainage.

Pedestal sinks or wall mounted sinks may do well in such an application to save space and eliminate the need for cabinets. Tankless and corner toilets can save some space also, but the soil pipe may need to be relocated.

Pocket doors or sliding doors may maximize the interior space without adding a door physically opening into the space — or out into the hallway.

Bath Temperature Setting/Scald Control

One way to avoid accidentally using water that is uncomfortably or dangerously hot in the bath or shower — and risking discomfort and possible injury — is by setting the hot water heater to a maximum temperature of 120°.

Most dishwashers and washing machines have the heating ability within them to create the temperature above this that they need to perform properly. So, a lower hot water temperature may be the solution for you and the others in your home — including visitors and houseguests.

Still, many people may prefer a hotter temperature for a shower, for disinfecting surfaces, or for washing dishes by hand. Just be careful with hotter water if you or others in your home have difficulty feeling hot temperatures in your hands or feet.

The safety and comfort solution here — and one regardless of ability or needs — is an easy-to-read digital temperature or scald control for the tub or shower. It can be set for the desired temperature to keep the water from getting any hotter than what is selected.

Depending on how handy you are as the homeowner or renter, you can do this yourself — or you can have a handyman, kitchen and bath designer, plumber, or remodeler do it for you.

Folding Shower Seats

Because of physical limitations, some people need to sit down routinely in order to use the shower and bathe comfortably and effectively. If this is the case, they should have a seat installed or integrated into the shower design.

However, as a component of universal design, a folding seat is a good strategy that offers safety, comfort, accessibility, and convenience for everyone — regardless of their ability or often they might need or want to use it.

This way, the seat can be available when needed but stored against the rear or side shower wall of the shower and out-of-the-way when it isn't in use.

In households where the seat is required all the time by one or more people, you can leave it fully deployed, or one can be built in. For people who require it occasionally, however, the folding seat can be opened into the operational position, used, and then stored again against the wall when they are finished.

This can be installed for bathtub use as well.

Overnight or longer-term houseguests can take advantage of the folding seat also. It is intuitive and available to be deployed and used.

It can be designed in a variety of sizes and materials — as long as they are suitable for a wet area and can be cleaned easily. Also. they can be installed in all of the bathrooms rather than just the master bath.

Whether it's sitting to let the water massage a muscle pull or general muscles aches (or sore feet), sitting to keep stitches or surgical sites in the lower leg or foot from getting wet, sitting because of fatigue or low stamina, sitting to shave your legs, or sitting while someone assists with the bathing, a fold down seat accommodates a wide range of users and can be used when necessary and stored away when it isn't needed.

Because it needs to be anchored securely into the wall, and ceramic tile or other hard surface shower surround materials are involved, you may want to have a remodeler, handyman, kitchen and bath designer, or durable medical equipment specialist do this job.

If the walls have had wooden wall blocking installed during an earlier remodeling project or the original construction (boards installed edgewise between the studs and flush with the front surface of them), this will facilitate the installation of the seat and allow more flexibility in choosing a location.

Built-In Shower Seats

For anyone who routinely need to sit down in order to use the shower or those who would rather have a built-in seat instead of a fold-down version, choose a built-in seat that is integrated into the shower design. This can be formed into an acrylic or fiberglass shower base along with the shower pan, or it can be constructed and tiled as part of the shower.

The fold-down seat is a good universal design treatment for multiple users in a household or for people who don't need to use it every time they shower or bathe. However, as a component of universal design, a permanently installed and built-in seat is also a good strategy for safety, comfort, and convenience — as long as it is designed and constructed well.

It needs to out-of-the-way so that it doesn't interfere with anyone entering and exiting the shower. It shouldn't be an impediment to passage or a potential tripping or bumping into hazard. It should not infringe on open access or the passageway into the shower.

It needs to be high enough to safely sit on it but not so high that it is uncomfortable or hard to use. If it is too low, there is a risk of falling while trying to sit on it.

Remember that it is going to be a tile surface so it will be hard and inflexible. Also. it needs to be designed so that it will drain well and not retain pooled water on it.

Make sure that it actually is built-in and tiled rather than just a wooden bench that is placed in the shower and not anchored.

While a wooden or plastic bench might make sense as far as moving it about in the shower or taking it out to clean it, it is unsafe because someone might trip on one of the legs (also true if someone leaves the folding seat deployed), it might interfere with safely entering the shower, and it could tip or slip if someone places their weight on it awkwardly. Keep this in mind when using or deciding on temporary transfer seats also.

If someone needs to transfer from a wheelchair to the built-in seat, make sure it is large enough and accessible enough to allow this — with grab bars as necessary.

Free-Standing Bathtubs

A common bathroom design trend is to use free-standing bathtubs in the master bathroom — located in the middle of the floor with nothing around them, or near a wall but not attached to the wall.

These are not universal design features. They present many safety issues and generally are not desirable to have in your home. They typically have tall sloping sides, and many are elevated from the floor on platforms, stands, or claw feet — making them even taller.

The risk of slipping getting in the tub — assuming your legs are long enough or you have sufficient flexibility in your hips and waist to climb over the edge of the tub — is high for anyone. Someone with poor balance, coordination, or range-of-motion — or someone who is short of stature — will find these tubs very hard to use.

They are aesthetically pleasing and add a decorator statement to a bathroom, but they are not functional for most people.

Since the tubs are located in the middle of the room (or sometimes next to a wall), there are no grabs bars or any other form of support to use in getting in or out of the tubs — nor on top of or inside the tubs. There are no steps to use getting into or out of the tub.

They are relatively large and deep so they necessarily would hold a tremendous amount of water if they were to be filled to capacity — more than the volume of just one typical hot water heater.

Floor Mounted Plumbing

When free-standing bathtubs are used, they often have a water supply at the front or side of the tub that is exposed (rather than hidden or enclosed under the tub), and this creates a tripping hazard for anyone that might walk too closely to it or not realize that it is there.

By eliminating or choosing not to install the free-standing tub, this issue will not be a concern. This is just another reason why these tubs are not a universal design product or practical for many homes.

Walk-In Bathtubs

At first glance walk-in tubs appear to be a great product for seniors or anyone else who might want to bathe in this fashion — they offer independence and privacy for those desiring a bathtub experience who cannot use a traditional bathtub easily.

However, they are not a universal design product because they aren't practical for all ages to use — even though there is nothing technically preventing anyone from using it who can walk into it and sit down. Mainly, they are not unobtrusive and are noticeable as a special feature — regardless of why they might be present.

While it might seem that walk-in tubs would allow seniors and others to use them without assistance, there are many potential drawbacks for including this feature in your home.

This is not a do-it-yourself project. It will require professionals to install it and hook up all of the plumbing. The fixture itself can run several thousand dollars not counting installation, depending on which one is selected — and whether it has water jets or a heating feature.

There are many designs, brands, styles, sizes, and shapes from which to choose. Some are taller and narrower than others. Some are longer and a bit lower. Some fit in the space where a regular tub was. All take a very large volume of water to use them comfortably — more hot water than can be delivered by a typical gas or electric hot water tank unless a tankless hot water heater is added also.

Depending on the type of tub selected, the amount of water to fill it to a comfortable soaking level can be more than twice that of a standard bathtub.

Thus, as the tub is filling the water will begin to cool (unless there is a heating element in the tub), and one's body will adjust to the water temperature so that it will seem cooler than it is. The only way to add more hot water is to stand up (often without a grab bar for assistance) and reach for the faucet. This poses many standing, slipping, sitting, and general comfort issues.

With any of the walk-in tubs, a person must enter them and secure the door before the water can be turned on and the temperature adjusted. Then they must sit there as the tub fills to the desired level.

They door cannot be opened again until the water drains to below the bottom surface of the door. It generally takes a couple of minutes to drain the tub.

Some of the cabinets have locking latches that take a certain amount of strength and the ability to push down forcefully. This could be an issue for some people who aren't tall enough or lack sufficient range-of-motion or hand, arm, or shoulder strength.

Most of the models available have a very limited amount of grab bars integrated into their design. Typically (but not always) there is one located inside the tub across from the door or on the back of the door, but almost none of them have a grab bar on the top edge or the outside of the tub near the door. There is no support or anything to grab onto to prevent a fall if someone should begin to slip as they are exiting or entering the tub.

Also many of the tubs have a fairly sizeable step up or down from the floor of the tub to the bathroom floor — plus a retaining lip to step over that the door closes against. This can be a significant safety issue.

Consider what each tub offers and then weigh any shortcomings or concerns before deciding which one to install or whether to have one at all. Then, if you do select one, make sure that it sized correctly for the needs of whomever will be using it and for the space where it is to be installed.

Safety will remain an on-going concern.

Soaking/Garden/Whirlpool Bathtubs

The soaking or garden tub (with or without whirlpool jets) was quite a popular feature in master bathroom designs for years, and builders offered them in new construction across a range of price points. Now the free-standing tub seems to have become just as popular, and I already discussed this feature.

Many people find that stepping into and climbing from a soaking tub can present many safety and comfort challenges. As a result, the tub sits there unused — occupying a very large part of the bathroom area.

Add to that the amount of water used to fill the tub, and the fact that the water tends to cool off quickly (to the extent that a heating element, if used, helps mitigate this) — these are issues that I mentioned for both the free standing tubs and the walk-in tubs also.

Handheld/Personal Showers

The handheld or personal shower is a great universal design strategy that offers safety, comfort, and convenience for anyone.

It can be an auxiliary showering device to an existing fixed showerhead or the only showering fixture in a bathtub or stall shower.

It may be mounted along a slide bar to rest on or in a holder or cradle, or it might retract into the tub fixture.

When the handheld or personal shower is mounted along a slide bar where it rests in a cradle attached to the slide bar, and the height of it can be adjusted up or down along the length of the bar, some people may choose to leave it in place at the selected height and just use it as a wall-mounted shower. Others will remove the shower wand from the mount and hold it.

When a folding or stationary shower seat is used, the handheld shower — with sufficient hose length — can easily be used by someone while they remain seated. Just make sure that a sufficiently long hose is installed for this purpose — and that it remains unkinked and out of the way to avoid tripping or getting tangled in it regardless of how long the hose is.

When bathing assistance is required — or when just a particular skin area needs to be washed or conversely remain dry — the handheld offers good flexibility.

The main safety concern with a handheld (aside from the hose being a tripping hazard) is the way it is mounted for storage on the wall. There are slide bars that are being manufactured as dual purpose grab bars and slide bars — even with small diameters — and these are great.

Make sure to look for such a slide bar with the ability to be used as a grab bar in an emergency because it will be used as such anyway — even if it's not designed or intended to be used that way — just because it is there.

In existing applications where a handheld shower already exists but with a slider or mount that is not designed to double as a grab bar, change it out with one that is designed for this purpose — and with stronger screws or anchors — so it can withstand a panic grab or offer additional support when needed.

Adding a handheld shower can be a relatively simple do-it-yourself project, but a handyman or remodeler can do it as well.

Towel Bars/Hooks/Rings

This is a major safety concern in bathrooms.

Just as slide bars for a handheld or personal showers are not designed to be used as grab bars unless they are specifically manufactured and installed for this dual purpose of being a slide bar and a grab bar, towel bars generally are not designed to be used for support either.

Nevertheless, many towel bars and rings — especially those installed near or inside the tub or shower space — are used as a grab bar in a panic. When someone loses their balance and slips, they look for the first thing they can find to support their weight or break their fall. The towel bar looks like it will work.

Unfortunately, many towel bars will break when sufficient downward or gripping pressure is applied to them — such as during a panic fall — or they may pull lose from the wall. They are only designed to support a few towels and not someone's full body weight or downward force as they are falling.

Even if the bars or rings don't actually break from the added pressure of someone trying to use them for support, they easily can pull lose from the wall. Either way, they will fail to support someone — essentially because they are not designed for this emergency purpose. It is not a fault of the towel bars or rings.

Nevertheless, there are towel bars specifically designed to be used as grab bars also.

An important safety consideration when a towel is on the bar, rod, or ring is that someone may grab it rather than the bar, and the towel may slip off the bar and defeat the intended purpose. This issue is heightened when the towel bars are installed near the tub or shower.

For overall safety, comfort and convenience, towel bars should be mounted away from the actual shower or bath area so that they are not mistakenly or expediently used for support. Use actual grab bars — not towel bars — in and around your tub and shower areas and do not put towels on them.

Sometimes towels hooks are used, but these do not tend to keep the towels on them very well and can cause injury if someone falls against them — or slips or trips on the towel that has fallen to the floor.

Changing out towel bars or moving them generally can be handled by the homeowner or renter unless you don't feel comfortable undertaking a job such as this, it's part of a more comprehensive remodeling project that you are undertaking, or drilling through ceramic tile or marble is involved. Just remember that they need to be anchored well into the wall in order to be effective as a grab bar.

Strategic Grab Bars

People tend to associate grab bars in a residential setting with people requiring them due to age or a specific need. However, they do serve a useful universal design function when used as a positive strategy, and anyone (regardless of age) can benefit from them.

I call this concept "strategic grab bars" because I think for safety, comfort, and convenience, a well-designed, well-located, and attractive grab bar should be positioned vertically near the entrance to every tub or shower — at a suitable height for use by everyone in the household (or at least those who would typically use that particular bathtub or shower).

I think that everyone at least once in their lifetime has needed a little extra support getting in or out of the tub or shower — possibly because they slipped or lost their balance getting in or out of the tub or shower.

Perhaps they had an injury or recent surgery that kept them from putting their full weight on the ground, or they got a muscle cramp or spasm (in their leg, foot, or back) that interfered with their ability to stand or put their entire weight on their feet.

Maybe they were generally sore from exercise or other activity or just like knowing that something is there.

The strategic grab bar (or strategically placed grab bar, if you prefer) is a good universal design feature that can be incorporated into an aesthetically pleasing look.

Anyone in your home can use it, regardless of age or ability, and your houseguests will appreciate seeing it and being able to use it as they need it also.

One grab bar per tub or shower is likely sufficient as a strategic grab bar. For functional grab bars, you will want to add at least one more.

"Pseudo" Grab Bars

While including a vertical strategic grab bar on the wall at the back edge of a tub or shower (typically the one away from the shower head), make sure you also look for and remove all "pseudo-grab bars" or de-facto ones.

Replace anything that looks like someone might grab onto it or reach for it for support when they slip — that really was never designed to function that way. This includes towel bars, soap dishes, toothbrush holders, or anything similar in the bath or shower area that might be grabbed by someone in a panic situation (regardless of its size or shape).

This would also include removing any grab bars mounted with suction cups. They simply cannot be relied upon to work when needed.

If these other fixtures and items are located in a convenient location, then replace them with something that is specifically designed to provide the required support. Otherwise, just remove them and patch or paint where they were and don't put anything else in its place.

Grab bars must be designed to hold up to the pressure and force applied to them, and they must remain anchored to the wall. They must be structurally sound and up to the task.

Because of the safety factor involved here, you want to make sure that all grab bars are installed properly, so a handyman, kitchen and bath designer, or remodeler may be the appropriate one to do it.

Functional Grab Bars

Strategic grab bars are universal. Everyone can use them, and they blend into any design without calling undue attention to them.

"Pseudo" grab bars are dangerous and need to be removed — or replaced with something more substantial that actually is created and designed to function as a grab bar.

That brings us to adding grab bars that can be installed as needed or desired for a specific purpose.

They won't be universal in the sense that they are totally unnoticeable, but in another way, they will roughly appear to be about the same as existing towel bars and other bathroom accessories that people have come to use as grab bars anyway in an emergency.

Be sure to design for yourself and your own needs. The two grab bars that typically are installed along the side wall and rear wall of a toilet location are totally impractical although they meet ADA guidelines.

The bar behind the toilet serves no purpose at all in assisting someone to stand. The one on the side is roughly shoulder height when you are seated so it requires a lot of shoulder, chest, tricep, bicep, forearm, hand, and abdominal muscle strength (at a minimum) as well as good range-of-motion to be able to pull oneself into a standing position from a very awkward leverage standpoint.

Because residences are exempt from ADA requirements unless specifically demanded by your local building code, ignore the height recommendations and suggested locations. Go with a placement that makes sense for you and the ones in your home who will be using them.

One more thing about positioning the grab bars. The strategic grab bars at the entrance to the tub or shower should be mounted vertically.

The slide bars for the handheld showers also will be vertical although most of the other grab bars will be installed horizontally and parallel to the floor. There are "L" bars as well that are a one-piece combination of both a vertical and horizontal bar.

There is a school of thought that likes to install grab bars on a diagonal with the thinking that this gives someone plenty of chances to grab the bar multiple at heights rather than locate it just in one position. This is more appropriate near a toilet than in a tub or shower location — and for pulling oneself up onto a wheelchair or into a standing position rather than preventing a fall.

In grabbing a diagonal device when your hands are wet, you may very well slip along it and ride it to its lowest point. The same thing could happen on a vertical bar, but they tend to be shorter in overall length.

Therefore, a horizontally mounted bar (or "L" bar) is the best choice for supporting you at the point where it is grabbed — especially in wet areas.

Tilt-Out/Tip-Out Sink Front Bins

In the kitchen and baths (and occasionally in the laundry room), an area that goes unused that can be a great universal design strategy is the cabinet blank in front of the sink — one or two depending on the design, and with or without dummy drawer pulls.

For convenience and efficiency, these can be turned into functioning, safe access, tilt-out or tip-out storage bins or trays — depending on their depth. Otherwise, they remain unused storage potential.

In the bath, they will replace medicine cabinets that tend to go unused because they are often are hard to reach. The bins will bring handy, everyday grooming, hygiene, and other small useful items right to your fingertips. This saves reaching for them and possibly dropping them also.

People of any age or ability can use these bins as they require very little effort to pull them open, don't latch but stay in place with tension hinges, and don't have a particularly large capacity so weight is usually not a concern.

The main safety concern would be keeping sharp items (such as razor blades, scissors, sewing needles, syringes, and tweezers), medicines and pain relievers (prescription or over-the-counter), and other dangerous or unsuitable items from such bins if you have small children in your home or are likely to have young grandchildren visiting you.

Depending on how complicated it is to get the blank cabinet fronts off and replace them with the bins, this could easily be a do-it-yourself project. Certainly a handyman or remodeler could do it.

If you are replacing cabinets, look for ones where this design strategy can be employed. There may not be enough room to use this technique with undermount or integrated bowl sinks because of the limited space between the cabinet and the edge of the sink bowl so check for available room first.

Body Dryer

This is very high-tech, modern, and state-of-the-art appliance — and it's a great universal design strategy. It provides safety, comfort, convenience, and it is highly accessible.

It's a heated, forced air, electric dryer for use after showering. It is mounted in a corner of the shower and provides a series of heated air jets to blow dry anyone standing or seated in front of it much the same way that hair dryers or automatic hand dryers do.

They are said to take about the same amount of time that a person uses to towel dry, but towel drying does not remove all of the water like these do.

People with range-of-motion issues or those who might need help drying themselves would find this fixture useful, but anyone could use it to make sure they get completely dry. It's also a great conversation starter when houseguests or friends see it, and it is quite sanitary and saves on laundering towels.

This is specifically designed for use in a wet area so it is safe. It needs to be hardwired into the electrical circuit rather than just being plugged in. You may need an electrician, handyman, or remodeler to install it.

Toe-Kick Lighting

The toe kick — that little recess of a few inches tall by a few inches deep that keeps the base cabinets in the kitchen, bathroom, or laundry room from resting directly on the floor and gives people a place to put their feet to maintain their balance while in front of the cabinets — can be put to effective use with additional ambient lighting in the form of LED rope lighting, fluorescent strip lighting, xenon strip lighting, or LED strip lighting.

This takes advantage of an otherwise unused space to provide general illumination for more safety in the room where it is used. It makes a great night or early morning light and helps out in low-light situations when overhead or other lights are not on or available.

Depending on what type of lighting is selected and where the electrical outlet or electricity source happens to be, this might be as simple as plug-it-in-and-use it. It also can be installed with a dimmer control if desired. It can be switched, used with a timer or photo cell, or just left on because of its energy efficiency.

Under-Cabinet/Task Lighting

The kitchen requires a variety of lighting sources since there are so many different types of tasks going on there. In addition to the toe-kick area, another underutilized area of the kitchen (and the bath and laundry room) for installing additional lighting is the area under the upper cabinets.

As is the case for toe-kick lighting, adding lighting under the upper cabinets might be a simple plug-in-and-use installation that you can do. It could require the services of an electrician or low voltage electrical contractor or electrical services contractor — depending on where the electrical outlet or electricity source happens to be and if a new connection or outlet has to be installed. This could also be part of a larger kitchen (or bath) remodeling project.

This strategy and universal design treatment provides additional countertop, workspace, and indirect ambient lighting for the kitchen, bath, laundry room or other are where it is used.

The lighting can be switched, used with a timer, or just left on because of its energy efficiency — LED rope lighting, fluorescent strip lighting, xenon strip lighting, or LED strip lighting. This also makes a great night or anytime fill-in light and helps out in low-light situations when overhead or other lights are not switched on.

This is a solution that provides additional safety and convenience by adding more light to the countertop work and prep surface and to the room in general. Just make sure that it doesn't create any glare on the countertop or small appliances.

Overhead & General Lighting

At one time, homes were built with ceiling light fixtures in every room. You might remember seeing them, or you might have such a home currently.

While the centralized ceiling fixtures often delivered harsh, localized lighting that could cast strong shadows and didn't fill the entire room with effective lighting, each room at least had this light source. Often the fixture size in terms of the number of bulbs it contained and the wattage output was insufficient to adequately light the room.

For older homes where this style of lighting is still being used (where the ceiling fixtures haven't been removed or replaced with an updated one) and for newer homes where foyers, living rooms, dining rooms, bedrooms, kitchens, baths, hallways, stairways, laundry rooms, porches, patios, garages, closets, or basements may have ceiling light fixtures also, the light output might be insufficient for the activity in the room or space — making this a safety, convenience, and comfort issue.

Depending on the size, shape, design, type, and age of the ceiling lighting fixtures you have in your home, and the number and wattage of bulbs they can support, it may be possible to increase the light output to be more effective. Otherwise, a new fixture that provides more light may be the solution.

Just be aware that shadows and glare caused by brighter overhead lights may affect vision and depth perception and be a comfort and safety concern.

The older we get, we generally need more lighting to read and perform other tasks than we did when we were younger — lighting that is illuminating the page we are trying to read or the task we are working on rather than just general lighting of a space.

To supplement overhead lighting, you can use table lamps and floor lamps in bedrooms, living rooms, dining rooms, home offices, basements, porches, family rooms, and other living areas — again paying attention to the light output, shadows, glare, and "hot spots."

In living rooms, dining rooms, family rooms, bathrooms, and bedrooms, wall lamps or sconces offer supplemental lighting but generally not enough to light a large area.

In kitchens and bathrooms, the toe-kick and task lighting are great supplemental lighting sources.

While consumers can change out light bulbs rather easily, you may or may not feel confident in replacing light fixtures and choose to rely on a family member of the services of a handyman, electrician, or remodeler. Using a professional would be especially helpful if a new receptacle, wall switch, or circuit needs to be installed or the fixture is particularly large or heavy.

Many ceiling fans come with light kits — optional or already installed. This provides a central ceiling lighting resource also, but the light output, intensity of the light, glare, and shadows cast may be similar to other ceiling fixtures.

Light Bulb Choices

The types of light bulbs available for consumers to use in lamps, ceiling fixtures, and elsewhere around the home has changed rather dramatically in recent years and continues to evolve.

Incandescent bulbs largely have been phased out. The CFL's (compact florescent bulbs) have numerous safety, health, and practical concerns involved with using them. They contain mercury, may not fit well in the lamp socket or lighting fixture, can be unattractive due to their shape and size, and may present health risks.

Regular florescent tubes and rings (with less safety and health issues than CFL's but still some present) and halogen bulbs (although they produce a lot of heat and can cause a burn) can still be used.

However, LED lighting is the trend of the future. LED light bulbs tend to cost more initially but last several years, can be used with a dimmer, do not put out any appreciable heat, are being manufactured in higher wattage outputs (what we normally think of as wattage), and are more widely available than they were — and in more styles and sizes.

The prices are dropping, and the market is getting quite competitive.

As we move to LED lights, we need to re-educate ourselves to choose the correct bulb. The traditional measurement of a bulb's brightness and light output for years has been wattage — 40w, 60w, 75w, and 100w, for instance.

Now, with the LED bulbs, we are more concerned with lumens (the amount or intensity of light produced) and color temperature (such as daylight, warm white, cool white) than with what particular wattage it is.

The LED does not produce as much light as an incandescent bulb of the same equivalency, but the lack of heat produced, the considerably lower energy consumption, and the length of time they last make LED's a much better choice than incandescent bulbs.

Ceiling Fans

Ceiling fans, in addition to providing comfort and air circulation, can also function as ceiling light fixtures when the light kits are installed on them — as an optional feature or as part of the original package.

They can supplement other ceiling or wall-mounted light fixtures that you might have and can provide a central ceiling light for your room when none other exists (with one or more bulbs mounted in the center of the fan under the blade motor) or an array of several bulbs extending from the center.

Keeping lights and fans dusted (for air quality and general appearance) and avoiding a strobing effect (to keep the fan from creating a pulsing light pattern on the walls, ceiling, floors, or furniture) are the main issues with ceiling fans and the lights attached to them.

Some homeowners or tenants can install their own ceiling fans (or add a light kit to an existing fan) as long as they have the physical ability and range-of-motion and dexterity to lift a somewhat heavy and awkward fan into position, maintain their balance, hold it in place while the wiring is connected, and attach it to the mounting hook or screws.

Otherwise, a handyman, electrician, carpenter, or remodeler can do this.

Skylights

In any room where additional overhead lighting is desired — primarily during daylight hours — skylights are a good choice. They can provide more illumination.

As long as they are installed properly so that there are no leaks, they are sized right for the space (a major universal design precept), and they are not shadowed excessively or blocked by overhanging tree branches (an occasional branch blowing in the breeze may be OK), skylights (when ceiling space and rafters accommodate or allow their use) can be an effective supplemental (and free) lighting source. They are sustainable and use no energy.

Also, they will reduce the energy demand for other lighting during daylight hours so there is an additional economic benefit as well. There is no direct cost to use them as a light source (after they are installed) and they save money by reducing the need for other lighting to be on.

Skylights come in square and rectangular shapes with either flat or domed lenses — fixed and well as being able to be opened and closed with a motor. They also come round with polished steel tubes connecting a ceiling lens or diffuser with the roof lens or collector (available in a variety of diameters and from various manufacturers).

The round skylights also have light kits so that they can double as a ceiling light during evening hours or other times when supplemental room lighting is needed.

This project definitely will require the services of a remodeler, carpenter, handyman, roofer, or skylight installer — and possibly an interior designer, architect, and electrician (for the light kit) — to make sure the skylights are located correctly, the roof and ceiling are cut in the right place, the alignment is made with the ceiling location, everything is trimmed out properly, and that there are no leaks.

Eye-Level Controls

This is a universal design element that addresses accessibility, comfort, convenience, and safety issues in your home.

Often the wall-mounted controls in a home, such as thermostats and switches for ceiling fans (and even some light switches) are mounted higher than eye level (making them hard to see and use easily) or beyond the easy reach of children, a short adult, or a person in a wheelchair. However, regular light switches typically are located at a reasonable height.

Controls in any room that are located generally less than 48" (4 feet) above the floor surface allow the widest range of accessibility and usage.

Thus, by lowering the switches and controls, a small adult (or child), those who might be in a wheelchair, those who might have physical limitations that keep them from standing erect (including those requiring support from a cane or walker), and those with range-of-motion issues in their elbows or shoulders that prevent a normal arm extension could reach them — in addition to those of average or above average height who actually could reach something mounted higher.

Sometimes mixing or distribution valves in tubs and showers, the digital displays and controls for wall ovens and microwaves, and exhaust fan switches and work lights on range hoods fall into this same category of being mounted higher than easily accessible or visible in terms of being able to use them easily — and safely.

If wall controls are placed in the general vicinity of light switches, they would be more convenient and aesthetically pleasing than having them take up more wall space and not be as centrally located on your wall.

If the wiring going to the controllers or devices is long enough to allow relocating or moving them without any rewiring, this could be a do-it-yourself project for you. Of course, the walls would need to be patched and repainted where the former installations were.

An electrician, handyman, or remodeler may need to do this work — especially if there is not enough wire going to the controller or switch to allow it to be moved without running more wiring or you don't feel comfortable with working around electrical wires.

Electrical Outlets

Depending on the building codes in effect where you are, the standard location of an electrical outlet from the floor is likely fine — as long as it's not actually in the floor where it can create a tripping or stumbling hazard when it is used.

However, installing standard electrical receptacles higher than usual above the floor so they are in easy reach of everyone is a good universal design strategy as long as they are not so high as to call attention to their placement by looking unusual.

In some rooms such as kitchens, bathrooms, and laundry rooms, the outlets tend to be higher anyway — just over the height of countertops or adjacent to them. Sometimes, they are mounted in the sides of the base cabinets if they are accessible in the room.

In rooms such as bedrooms, outlets can be a little higher because furniture often hides them and makes them difficult to access when installed closer to the floor.

The height from the floor that outlets normally are placed is not inconsistent with the ADA guidelines (9" for direct access by a person in a wheelchair and 18" for someone reaching out for it from a wheelchair position), but if they were installed a little higher, more people could reach them easier without bending so much — generally safer to do.

This would include taller adults, people using a walker, people with range-of-motion issues, and those who have difficulty bending down or standing up again.

Depending on how many outlets need to be moved and how sufficient the wiring is going to the various outlets, this could be a do-it-yourself project. Attic or basement access might be necessary as well. The walls would need to be patched and repainted where the former boxes were.

An electrician, handyman, or remodeler may need to do this work — especially when there is not enough wiring to move the boxes without running more wiring.

Wall-Mounted Mirrors

All homes need mirrors, and most homes have several of them — generally found in bathrooms, bedrooms, and foyers or hallways.

Many are decorative mirrors — regardless of their size or shape — that are framed and hung on the wall like a picture.

Some mirrors, such as those in bathrooms, are large and mounted directly to the wall with adhesive or clips. Others are considered to be "full-length" and attached to the back of a door.

Still others are used as bypass or bi-fold closet door panels.

The way that mirrors become a universal design concept and strategy is when they are accessible and usable by everyone in the home.

They don't necessarily have to be a tilted mirror that adjusts on a pivot (aiming somewhat downward with the top of the mirror being further from the wall than the bottom), but this can be a universal design treatment if everyone in the home can use the mirror comfortably and see themselves in it.

Generally, the height at which tilting or fixed mirrors are mounted and the focal length created by the installation (particularly with a tilted mirror) means that the mirrors are mounted too high to see more than just your head and upper torso.

Mirrors mounted behind the sink are generally no lower than 30" unless the countertop is lower. Often mirrors are higher than this because of a clearance space allowed between the countertop and the bottom of the mirror. Design and function often are at odds.

This is true even when there is a sit-down vanity.

Additionally, there usually there is a wall opposite the wall-mounted mirror that keeps someone from backing up far enough to get a longer vertical view and see themselves effectively.

Even when you get a full body view from a wall-mounted mirror, the distance is such that you are quite far from the mirror. Then, being able to see much detail for grooming or choosing an outfit becomes an issue.

Lighting above or around the mirrors further affects the functionality of the mirrors due to glare, "hot spots," insufficient lighting, shadows, and the color temperature of the bulbs.

Full-length and closet door panels offer a much better (and safer to use) solution than wall-mounted mirrors because they accommodate any physical size.

A small child, a person in a wheelchair, a basketball player, or anyone else can all see themselves in such mirrors. Rather than moving back to see more of yourself (as is the case with most mirrors), you actually can get as close as necessary to the mirror.

In selecting mirrors, pay attention to the weight of the mirrors relative to where they will be installed or used, how you intend to mount them, the likelihood of the mirrors beginning to de-silver along the edges, and the general quality of the glass so imperfections are avoided. Nevertheless, mirrors are relatively inexpensive to purchase.

Some homeowners and renters can handle a project of this nature (especially if someone else can help you hold and support part of the mirror while you are installing it), but a professional can do this easily. In addition to being somewhat heavy, mirrors are glass and can have sharp edges.

Visual Indicators

I have already mentioned visual clues to indicate relative water temperatures and to show where light switches and other controls are located. There also are other visual indicators that are universal design concepts and effective to have in your home.

For the hearing impaired, doorbells and telephones are often connected to one or more lights throughout the home that flash when someone rings the doorbell or calls on the phone, but this concept can benefit anyone.

The lights might be in the living room, kitchen, bedroom, or other areas of the home.

They are a great feature for anyone (and thus universal in concept) because they provide another — and silent —

way of alerting us to the presence of someone at the front door or on the phone (for those people who have a landline).

With all of the noise present in a home from time-to-time — from TVs, music players, computer videos, conversation, appliances, vacuum cleaners, fans, air conditioners, and other devices — having a visual way of knowing when someone is at the door or calling on the phone would help everyone.

There are traffic, airplane, machinery (such as lawn mowers), and other outside noises present at various times also.

Small children (if there are any present) could easily see and recognize the visual signal, as could anyone else in the home.

This is a feature that offers safety, comfort, and convenience to any home.

There are some easy-to-install kits that can be obtained from electronic stores for you to install yourself. Otherwise, an electrician, handyman, ESC (low-voltage electrical services contractor), or remodeler can do this job for you.

5

More Universal Design Safety & Convenience Strategies

More Universal Design Strategies For Safety, Convenience, Comfort And Accessibility

There are several other universal design strategies, treatments, and recommendations that we should look at that positively impact the overall safety and quality of life in your home.

Many design concepts and solutions can be used as part of a more comprehensive remodeling than just changing out a few fixtures or moving the location of various controls.

The focus with any renovation, design change, or home improvement should be increasing the comfort, safety, convenience, and accessibility for those in your home.

Some of the concepts that we are going to look at in this chapter are going to have wider appeal and interest for you than others, but all can be effective. Most of them are true universal design and are included because of the additional safety benefits they provide.

These strategies will require some advance planning and consultation. In some cases, major changes are involved.

The issue is not whether they are good design or will make your home safer and more comfortable but whether you want to incorporate them (and which ones) in any renovation projects that you are doing or planning.

Budget, time to complete them, and how to undertake the various projects are considerations in deciding how and where in your home to get started.

Contrast And Glare

As part of the normal aging process, we need more light to read and to see objects close up that we want to examine the older we get. Everyone faces this fact of life.

At the same time as we might need more light to read or examine objects closely as we get older, however, our eyes also tend to be more affected by bright lights and glare. We are more susceptible to misjudging distances and determining how close objects are that might be in front of us.

Another issue that can affect balance, orientation, and depth perception is visual clutter or confusion brought on by busy or repetitive patterns in wallpaper or furnishings.

Therefore, two strategies that are effective for eliminating glare or confusion about surfaces and where objects are located are the use of color or contrast and using less shiny, reflective, or busy surfaces and patterns.

I already mentioned color and visual indicators with respect to hot and cold running tap water. Using red knobs on stove or cooktop fronts is a similar strategy.

Shiny surfaces such as window glass, mirrors, glass or polished metal panels in appliances, glass top tables (coffee tables, end tables, and breakfast or dinette tables) and glass shower enclosures (if you haven't removed them yet) — as well as hard surfaces such as countertops, appliance fronts (unless they have a matte finish), cooktops, and ceramic and polished hardwood flooring — are especially prone to reflecting light sources and creating glare when overhead lights are used. Sometimes natural light can do this also. Often where someone is standing in the room is a factor in how much glare is perceived.

Foil or other shiny wallpaper in bathrooms or laundry rooms can create "hot spots" from lights in those rooms or the way sunlight reflects off them. Glossy walls and other painted surfaces can do this as well. This is like the glare from the sun on a car windshield where all you can see is a bright light with no details of what is behind it.

Sometimes it's not even the sheen or glare that adds to our visual confusion and orientation but the busyness of patterns in a room can create the issue. Certain wallpaper, mosaic floor or wall tile, or patterned artwork can impact orientation and affect balance if it has a particularly repetitive or busy pattern.

In kitchens, people often like to use a monochromatic look to create an aesthetically pleasing appearance — where the cabinets, flooring, and appliances all have a similar color, hue, or finish — but this is not the best design for universal accessibility, safety, and comfortable use. It needs to be obvious where countertops and floors are located and not just have them blend from one surface to another.

A technique for defining showing where countertops are located is something called "edge-banding" where a contrasting color is used on the edge of the countertops to show where the countertop surface begins. Doing this with some hard surfaces such as granite or quartz will take more effort and will add to the cost, but it will make the kitchen safer.

Just having the countertop edges or surface be a different color while everything else in the room is a similar color or hue will not be enough to add a safe amount of contrast. Your eyes must be able to distinguish various surfaces and features in the room. This is commonly a kitchen issue but can be found in bathrooms, bedrooms, and laundry rooms also.

As for the flooring, toe-kick lighting that I already mentioned will illuminate part of the floor to show its location relative to the cabinets and reduce glare as well.

Be aware of furnishings also that there is sufficient contrast between the various furniture pieces, wall color, flooring, and accessories to create a safe, accessible, and easily navigable environment.

Listello

Listello is a border tile or pattern (although it can be wallpaper or other materials that serve the same purpose). It enhances safety by allowing our eyes to see something more specific in a large expanse of similarity.

It helps with reducing glare and improving orientation.

Normally it is used in ceramic or glass tile backsplashes or shower surrounds (as a smaller or contrasting tile and color) as a way of breaking up the large coverage of tile and adding visual interest. It gives our eyes something on which to focus.

It can also be used on flooring — tile (ceramic, porcelain, or vinyl) or hardwood (parquet or a different stain color) — to break up a long run of flooring or to differentiate spaces in the home where no doorways or walls exist to separate two adjacent rooms (such as the living room and dining area).

The important thing to keep in mind for using listello on walls is that it needs to be at eye level or a little below. If it's too high, it is ineffective and looks out-of-place.

Flooring

While flooring is a matter of personal choice and taste, there are types of flooring that tend to be more problematic than others for air quality, maintenance, sustainability, accessibility, comfort, and safety.

There are universal design choices and strategies concerning flooring, and carpeting generally is not a good choice anywhere in your home — for various reasons.

Carpeting was once quite popular, and many homebuilders still include it, but when it gets wet from rain or snow being tracked onto it, or from outerwear, shoes, or umbrellas dripping onto it — or when the door is opened and the wind blows in the rain or snow — it tends to remain wet for a period of time (where it can mildew and develop and odor). Pets will track in the precipitation and dirt also.

Wet carpeting is more susceptible to attracting dirt — leaving noticeable dirty marks or stains that remain even after the area is dry.

Carpeting shows stains from food (especially ones with sauces, condiments, and gravies) and beverage spills (wine, fruit juice, Kool-Aid, coffee, tea, milk). It stains from pet accidents, blood from cuts, and anything else tracked or spilled onto it (oil, grease, mud).

Also, carpeting tends to off-gas, and it retains dirt and other pet and airborne allergens. More than other types of flooring, it develops noticeable wear patterns.

It presents air quality issues and typically needs replacing every few years. It also fades from the UV rays in sunlight and florescent lighting.

Carpeting needs constant vacuuming, steam cleaning, or shampooing to help it retain its look, but it is never really showroom clean again. Small, sometimes sharp objects (even hard or sharp plant material or seeds) can fall into the carpet and be unnoticeable until stepped on, sat on, or fallen on.

Hard surface flooring is the best to use in your home, but hardwood flooring or hardwood-like flooring (engineered wood, laminates, and bamboo) should not be used in wet areas. Moisture causes the grain to expand and contract and affects the seams and joints.

Laminates and engineered wood flooring do not breathe, so any water or liquid spilled on them will be trapped beneath them when it seeps through the joints and seams. While bamboo is water resistant (not waterproof), it is not recommended for use in areas where it could get wet.

Ceramic tile — especially the new reticulated tile that fits together tightly and requires very small grout joints — is a hard surface that holds up well to water, spills, and foot traffic. This reduces difficulties in getting wheels to travel over grout lines — from toys, luggage, carts, walkers, or wheelchairs.

Tile is available in a variety of sizes and colors to match the color palette of the room in which it is installed and fit the proportions of the room.

The main issue with ceramic flooring is safety — it can be slick or slippery when wet, shiny to the point of creating glare (as I already mentioned), and hard to get good traction for walking across safely or using an aid such as a cane or walker. In these cases, treads of some type or a smaller tile (with more grout areas) or a mosaic pattern that is inlaid in places will provide more traction.

Ceramic tile typically shows wear patterns less than other types of flooring.

For years, vinyl flooring was not that popular except for relatively small applications (kitchens, laundry areas, mud rooms, foyers, and secondary bathrooms), but it has made a comeback.

It generally is well accepted and comes in a variety of sizes, styles (some look like ceramic tile or wooden planking), patterns and colors. It offers some cushion so it is easier on the feet and legs when standing on it and comes in several sizes and installation options.

Another type of flooring material that seems to work well — especially in the kitchen — is the natural product cork. Cork is especially nice to stand on and helps to cushion dishes and glasses when they are accidentally dropped onto it. However, it does need to be sealed to guard against water penetration and stains.

Some homeowners will be able to accomplish flooring removal and replacement, but most will rely on handymen, flooring contractors, tile setters, or remodelers. It also depends on what is being removed as far as dust and debris.

There also is the issue of disposing of the removed product.

If you are removing tile that has been in place for years, approach it cautiously. It could have asbestos in the tile or in the mastic used to adhere it to the floor. If you suspect this is the case or you are unsure, have it evaluated before proceeding.

Area Rugs

While aesthetically beneficial, area rugs, throw rugs, carpet remnants, and runners are similar to carpeting in several respects and can be a slipping or tripping hazard — particularly when used in doorways between rooms or in the kitchen or bathroom in front of the sink.

Nearly everyone is susceptible to this danger, but vision difficulties may cause this to be more of an issue.

Also like carpeting, area rugs and similar coverings hold dirt and allergens. They generally can be laundered more frequently than carpeting and often can be washed in your automatic washing machine (depending on their size and weight). They can be heavy and awkward to handle, however (especially when they are wet).

Area rugs — depending on their size, thickness, and where they are used in the home — can get in the way of opening doors or moving items across the floor also.

Therefore, in maintaining true universal design principles, the use of area rugs and carpeting in the home should be discouraged for safety, air quality, maintenance, general comfort, and accessibility.

Automatic Dustpan

Keeping hard surface floors clean and tidy — for air quality, general appearance, and safety — requires constant attention. Picking up, vacuuming, or sweeping with a broom are daily activities to keep the floors presentable.

There are vacuums, electric brooms, and other devices that can be used, but they tend to be a little bulky, can be hard for some people to move them about, and generally require electricity to use them.

There are manual mops, brooms, and sweepers, but a device that is universal that may have application for you is the automatic dustpan.

A central vacuum system is required for this feature to work so a remodeling contractor or a central vacuum installer may be needed to accomplish this design. You also need the space to install it.

The primary safety aspect here is just allowing you to keep your hard surface floors as clean and dry as possible.

A central vacuum system is a great idea to have in the home, but it is not purely a universal design feature.

It offers convenience as far as being able to plug the hose into various wall ports located around the home instead of moving an upright or canister vacuum cleaner around the house, but it still requires some physical size, strength, range-of-motion, stamina, and coordination to be able to use it effectively.

The automatic dustpan port is a station connected to the central vacuum that is installed at floor level in the baseboard (available in various finished and colors). It is activated by a foot switch.

To use the dustpan port, simply sweep the floor and move the dust pile to the automatic dustpan where it can be vacuumed away into the holding tank. Of course, you or someone else in your home will need to be able to empty the vacuum tank occasionally.

Room-To-Room Transitions

When two different types or thicknesses of flooring meet in a doorway — or between rooms even without an actual doorway — an uneven transition between the two surfaces results, and it can present comfort, safety, and accessibility issues.

The same can be true for decks, porches, and stoops outside or at the entrance to your home.

Even when a molding strip (metal, wood, rubber, or vinyl) is used to separate two surfaces, going from one surface height (regardless of what it is) to another can present challenges for young children pushing toys along the floor, baby strollers, walkers, wheelchairs, and even furniture or carts on casters.

Walking from one surface to the other can even be a potential tripping or stumbling hazard for anyone who puts their weight down awkwardly on the higher or lower surface and twists their ankle or loses their balance. They might even catch the heel of their shoe or their toe (wearing shoes or not) on the molding and then stumble, lose their balance, or experience mild discomfort.

A uniform thickness of flooring — even if it's not the same product throughout the home — is the safe and comfortable way to handle this issue.

Depending on the number of instances where this exists in your home, it might be a do-it-yourself project to remedy the affected areas. More than likely, this type of project will need to be done by a remodeler or flooring contractor.

By replacing or redoing the flooring in most or all of your home, this issue will be eliminated. This would be a great opportunity to remove the carpeting and solve the additional issue of uneven transitions at the same time.

For transitions between indoor and outdoor spaces, look for ways to make the transition smooth with the smallest difference possible. Ideally the space can be bridged with a small ramp or otherwise made smooth so that an actual step up or down isn't necessary — even if there is no easy way to change the levels between the two surfaces.

Chair Rail

Chair rail or chair railing is a decorative molding that many people use in certain areas of their home (such as the dining room or hallway) or even throughout the entire home as an accent.

However, it can have a universal design application that will allow anyone who needs a little extra support to use it without it being a feature that calls attention to itself.

When someone enters a home and sees wooden or metal grab bars lining the hallway or other areas of the home because one of the occupants of that home needs them for support (in addition to or in place of a walker, cane, or other mobility assistance), it is obvious that this is a specialized installation as opposed to a universal design that is applicable to everyone.

Nevertheless, such a feature can be accomplished as a universal design with chair rail — generally installed about one-third of the distance up from the floor to the ceiling or some 32"-36" up toward an 8' ceiling. It can be a little lower or a little higher, but this range falls in line with ADA guidelines for the height of a grab bar anyway.

Chair rail is available in many different profiles, designs, and dimensions plus ones that can be created by combining two or more stock designs. It typically is installed parallel to the floor and flush against the wall surface. However, for use as an unobtrusive grab bar, install the chair rail with space between it and the wall.

Place a small board on the wall (1" x 3", 1" x 4", or 1" x 6") with a larger board attached directly to it. This outer board can either be a 1" board (typically only ¾" thick although it is called a 1" board although truly 1" lumber — called "five-quarter" or 5/4 — can be obtained and used for a little extra spacing between the outer board and the wall).

Then the outer board of either a 1" (actually ¾") or 2" (really 1½") thickness board (that is wider than the board attached to the wall) should be attached directly to the board that is touching the wall.

The outside board can have additional molding attached to it to make it look more decorative if you like, but it should have the top of it rounded (called "bull nose").

It can be painted a complementary but different color from the walls in that room, or it can be stained. Be sure to test fit it before installing it to determine that the person you are creating it for can grasp the railing and that their fingers will fit in the space between the inner and outer boards.

Adjustable Shelving

Sometimes the height differential between members in a household is so great that solutions are sought for accommodating the location of shelving or countertops in closets, kitchens, and other areas where people can access them easily and safely.

Even when shelves and countertops are installed at conventional heights, some people find that this is too high while others need them even higher. Of course, many people are fine with the typical installation.

For homes where there is a desire to accommodate this height differential or otherwise provide a higher or lower cabinet or closet shelf, or part of a countertop, for those using assistance such as a wheelchair, or to allow people to sit when preparing meals or grooming because of personal preference, stamina, circulation, or balance issues, a solution lies in adjustable shelving.

There are two ways to accomplish these adjustments: motorize them or create a manual solution.

The motorized approach may be more than you want to budget, but it works for anyone in your home. Simply push the controller to raise or lower a shelf or countertop portion, and it will move up or down to the desired position. When the person who moved it is finished, it can be returned to its normal position or allowed to remain where it is until the next time it is needed.

With the manual approach, this will take someone with the physical ability and strength (and range-of-motion) to reach and grasp the handle of the pull-down (above them or in front of them) or pull-up shelf or countertop unit (located at waist level or below them) and leverage it up or down into the desired position.

For this to work well, choose a shelving unit with gas pistons that assist and minimize the effort needed to operate it. They will also stabilize the movement so you don't lose control. Older style adjustable shelving systems have stiff tension springs that are much harder to operate and control.

This feature will work in a closet to move items around on a track or bring a shelf to within reach for convenience or accessibility.

It can be used in the bath or powder room to move a sink (vessel or one mounted in a small countertop) up and down as long as the water supply lines and drain tubing are flexible and installed with this in mind.

It can be used in the kitchen to provide comfortable and accessible eating space by moving a countertop section up or down. It also can be used to raise or lower cabinets, shelving, cooktops, and sinks.

A handyman, kitchen and bath designer, interior designer, remodeler, or electrician would be a good resource for accomplishing this — depending on the extent of the changes desired. Only for someone very experienced in do-it-yourself electrical and mechanical projects might this be done by the owner or tenant.

Kitchen Islands

In homes where there is an island as a feature in the kitchen, there could be safety, convenience, and access issues. Generally, islands tend to be too large for the kitchen floor space, and that presents issues.

People like the idea of having an island, but quite often there simply is not enough space around the island for two people to be in the same area at the same time, or for a cabinet or appliance door to open easily. Sometimes it's difficult for even one person to navigate the space around the island.

There needs to sufficient clear space — generally 48"-60" (four-five feet) — around each of the three or four sides of the island where cabinets, appliances, tables, passageways, or other functional areas of the kitchen or adjacent space (such as an eating area) are located.

It's not just a matter of someone in a wheelchair or walker being able to move around the island easily — although that certainly is a concern. This is a matter of general access and function as well as comfort, convenience, and safety.

Sometimes when the islands are really large for the kitchen space, it's tight for even one person to be in the kitchen and move around comfortably. Actions such as opening and using the microwave, cabinet doors and drawers, oven or cooktop, dishwasher, and refrigerator (or getting water or ice from the in-door dispenser) could be challenging. Two or more people in the kitchen at the same time only adds to the accessibility and safety demands.

Regardless of the size of the island — after it is adjusted to fall within acceptable clearance distances — all of the corners should be rounded with a radius sufficient to prevent injury from accidentally bumping into it while walking past or falling against it.

For universal design, if the resulting island is large enough for someone to sit down at it and eat — rather than just being a food preparation area or serving station — part of the countertop should be low enough and open enough to allow people to sit at it (or pull up a wheelchair) and eat. Remember to mark all the edges of the countertop to show the various heights.

Unless you are experienced with do-it-yourself projects of this magnitude, you likely will need the services of a handyman, kitchen and bath designer, interior designer, cabinet installer, remodeler, carpenter, electrician, or plumber — or several of them — depending on the extent of the changes needed.

Be careful not to use a rolling table as a substitute for an island. While it might be small enough to fit within the space guidelines, it presents additional challenges by possibly moving unexpectedly while someone is using it and being in the way when not in use.

Accessible Sinks

While having roll-in access to the kitchen or bathroom sinks is often desired, not everyone needs it. For this reason, it's not recommended as a universal design feature.

Nevertheless, as both a universal design and adaptable design feature, sink base cabinets in the kitchen and bathrooms can be designed and created intentionally to be removed later on as necessary — to create a more open look or to allow wheelchair access.

When the sink base cabinet is designed and created as a modular unit, it can be taken out completely (with those cabinets on either side of it remaining in place) to allow full access for someone in a wheelchair or just more open space for use with a chair or bench. This would not affect the integrity of the remaining cabinets or countertop.

It is universal because it shows no outward sign of being any different from the other cabinets at present, but it is easily adaptable when the time comes for a fully accessible sink by simply pulling the modular sink base unit out and removing it.

Also, a wall hung sink or a pedestal sink would allow wheelchair access without any other design changes required or necessary.

If it's just installing modular cabinets and securing them, a homeowner experienced in this type of job might do it. For the countertop, plumbing, and other aspects of this project, a remodeler, carpenter, plumber, electrician, or kitchen and bath designer may be needed.

Another universal design solution for providing wheelchair or open access to a sink is to create retractable doors on the sink base cabinet — the doors retract on a track or groove along the inside walls or ceiling of the cabinet much like the doors on a TV cabinet or entertainment center used to do.

It may not even be necessary to remove the toe-kick, but if that is desired, there are two way to handle this. It can be entirely removed (the riser and portion of the cabinet floor) and left off so that when the doors are opened and used in the retracted position, the place where the toe-kick normally is would be empty.

The cabinet floor also can be hinged and lifted up and raised back inside the cabinet (with the toe kick riser either coming with the floor or remaining in place).

Another solution is to remove the toe-kick and then to reconfigure the remaining cabinet floor. It can be designed as an plumbing access panel (when access is to the water supply pipes or trap is needed or desired) on a slant to provide open floor space in front of it, conceal the plumbing behind it, and have narrow open shelves on it for storing cleaning products and paper goods.

The doors need to be kept from moving inward past the flush closed position when not retracted. A stop, pin, cleat, or other device needs to be used to achieve this.

A homeowner experienced in woodworking type projects might be able to do this; however, a remodeler, carpenter, cabinet installer, or kitchen and bath designer may be needed.

Cabinets And Drawers

Cabinets (and closets) are a big focus of universal design because they are used in many rooms throughout the home, and storage is something everyone needs.

There are several other universal design strategies, solutions, and treatments involving upper and base cabinets — beyond what I already mentioned about the pulls, the tilt-out/tip-out bins, the lighting, the modifications to the sink base cabinets, and the adjustable shelving or tops.

There really are two main issues concerning cabinets: accessibility, ease of use, and the underlying safety.

In designing cabinets for replacement or in reworking existing cabinets — in the kitchen, bathrooms, basement, laundry room, linen closet, bedroom closets, garage, summer kitchen, mud room, patio, home office, dining room, hallways, or anywhere else they are located in the home — look at the size of the doors and drawers, the physical weight of the doors and drawers, the flexibility of using the storage space, the location of the door or drawer pulls on the actual doors or drawers, and the amount of room in front of them for someone to access them. Ease of retrieving items that are stored is a big, and very important, issue.

With drawers or pull-out shelves, bins, or baskets, the suspension system needs to provide sufficient support for the weight and easy movement of the drawers, shelves, bins, or baskets in and out — whether they are empty or loaded to capacity.

Thus, they should not be dependent on someone of any particular strength or ability being able to use them, and they should work equally well whether they are being accessed by someone from a standing, seated (such as on a chair, stool, bench, or wheelchair), or kneeling position.

Obviously, upper cabinets are tall and can go all the way to the ceiling (depending on the height selected and how high above the countertop they are mounted), but they should be designed so that most of the commonly used items are easily accessible and safely useable and retrievable at eye level or below.

Keeping the items most in demand and most frequently used at least one shelf up from the floor is part of this same strategy — to reduce the need for bending and straightening up again and for being able to access them from a seated position.

Another strategy for safely using upper cabinets without reaching is to install them actually resting on the countertop. While this concept makes them more accessible, it takes away useable counterspace that must be accounted for and accommodated elsewhere in the room — and it prevents using task lighting.

If there is an island — and it fits correctly in the kitchen with proper access all around it — it can provide the work and prep surface that is forfeited by having upper cabinets rest directly on the countertop.

An alternative to having the upper cabinets (some or all) resting on the countertops is to mount one or more upper cabinets lower than their traditional height but still up from the countertop a few inches — making them easier to reach than at their traditional height and preserving some countertop functionality (and the ability to use task lighting).

Another good idea is to look for smaller doors and cabinets so that a floor-to-ceiling linen, pantry, or supply cabinet can actually have two or more separate, smaller parts rather than a very tall closet-like cabinet — that would come with a necessarily heavier, larger, and harder-to-control door.

Some designers and consumers are returning to an open-look where just open wall shelves are used for storing or displaying cups, glasses, and dishware — in place of actual cabinets. There may or may not be upper cabinets used in conjunction with this design.

The openness certainly enhances accessibility; however, safety may be more of a concern as objects could fall or be knocked from the shelves.

Along this same line, open cabinets are being used that have no doors on them. Again, access is enhanced, but items knocked out or falling from the cabinet may present safety concerns. Also, keeping the dishware and glasses dusted is necessary since there are no doors to protect them. Clutter is another potential issue with open shelves.

Another concept that designers are using is to have all-drawer units in the base cabinets instead of doors that open with traditional shelving inside the cabinet. These allow you to organize and find like items in a drawer rather than bending down or reaching to access a shelf.

There are even corner drawer base units where the drawer fronts come together to form an interior 90° corner and the drawer comes out of the corner at a 45° angle. This brings items to the front and eliminates the blind corner or the need for a Lazy Susan for those not fond of this device.

Still, the drawers need to have a good suspension system that allows them to glide open and then close easily. Otherwise, the doors will work better — especially if hand or arm strength is an issue or concern. Also, the drawers — depending on their depth and the extent to which they are opened — could require more access room around them than opening a cabinet door.

Depending your ability and expertise, you may be able to do some or all of the work on the cabinets; however, the services of someone such as a handyman, remodeler, carpenter, kitchen and bath designer, architect, interior designer, or occupational therapist may be beneficial for an effective design and proper installation.

Countertop Heights

There are commonly accepted standards for countertop height, but they can be raised or lowered to make your life more comfortable, convenient, and safe.

There really isn't a good universal design standard for countertop height because one low enough to serve children and short adults would be too low for taller individuals, and countertops designed for taller people would be difficult for shorter people to use. That's why the adjustable countertop could be a good solution.

People with bad backs who can't bend at the waist very well might like a countertop higher than the traditional

36" kitchen counter or 29"-30" bathroom heights. In fact, a 36" bathroom countertop is fairly common except for sit-down vanities. Wheelchairs can generally access a 29" countertop height. This is the height of a typical desk.

On the other hand, people with osteoporosis can't stand erect and necessarily need a lower countertop height, and some people may need to sit on a stool, bench, or chair at the sink in the kitchen or bath in order to access them.

When one person in a household is much taller than the others, they might prefers a higher height for the countertop. Conversely, someone much shorter might like a lower height.

In the bathroom this can be accomplished with two vanities. In the kitchen, a single countertop height (whatever that might be) is generally chosen, but an adjustable countertop (motorized or manual) might be a solution for part of the kitchen.

Kitchen Desk

A sit-down desk in the kitchen) is a concept that many people already use that is installed inline in a base cabinet run or separately along another wall in the kitchen — as a standalone or along with other base cabinets (and often with upper cabinets or shelving.

Once marketed as a "recipe desk," it now serves as the more commonly referenced "kitchen desk" and is a great universal design concept that has multiple uses for a variety of ages and abilities.

However, the kitchen area may need to be enlarged or reconfigured to allow the use of the kitchen desk — depending on where you want to use it and how you want it located in the room.

The sitting area of the desk can be entirely open with just a countertop covering the space — inline with other cabinets so that the desk space is virtually invisible.

It also can look more like a typical desk with a single desk drawer beneath the countertop — or two or more adjacent drawers (depending on the width of the opening or knee space).

The drawer or side-by-side drawers under the countertop may interfere with sitting at the desk, so sufficient lap and leg room would need to be factored in for use with a desk chair, kitchen chair, stool, or wheelchair.

The design can also have one or two of the drawer base cabinet units on either or both sides of the knee space much like a traditional desk.

The countertop can be the same height as the other countertop space in the kitchen, but it is more versatile at a lower height in the 30" range — or even at the 29" typical desktop height.

Since this is a fairly common feature in many kitchens, the design does not suggest anything unusual, and it fits right in. Still, it allows wheelchair access as well as the ability for anyone else in the household (including young people doing their homework or playing games) to use this space.

It can be designed or used as a computer or TV/movie station (with a TV, desktop computer, notebook, or tablet) or just remain an open countertop for crafts, writing, meal planning, eating, meal or baking preparation (where doing it from a seated position is necessary or desired). It can even serve as an area for cooking or snack preparation with a small appliance (coffee maker, crockpot, toaster oven, microwave, popcorn popper, or induction burner).

Depending on the size of the desk you want to create (unless you already have one), and whether you want it to be a freestanding unit or inline with other base cabinets and the main countertop, you can purchase the cabinets and countertops from the home center store and install them yourself.

Otherwise, the services of a remodeler, carpenter, handyman, kitchen and bath designer, or interior designer will be required.

Sit-Down Vanity

This is similar in design and concept to the kitchen desk and has been used in the master bathrooms of many homes for years. It has never gone out of style, and you may already have one of these in your home — even if you don't use it that much or at all.

Like the kitchen desk, the sit-down vanity can be installed inline in a vanity base cabinet run or separately along another wall in the bath — as a standalone. It provides a safe way to sit while grooming, dressing, or applying makeup.

Also like the kitchen desk, the sit-down vanity can be entirely open with just a countertop covering the space, or it can have one or more desk drawers immediately under the countertop (depending on the width of the opening — knee space).

It can even be built to look like a desk with vertical drawer units installed along one or both sides of the knee space. Again, the drawer may interfere with sitting or wheelchair access so make sure there is enough space.

As a universal design feature, the sit-down vanity, which is typically installed in the master bathroom (or occasionally in a dressing area near the bath), can also be used in the guest or secondary bathrooms for your children or houseguests to use for their grooming needs.

A typical desktop height is 29" and many bathroom vanities are built to this height. They range all the way up to 36". Some people like the sit-down portion of the vanity to be at the same height as the rest of the bathroom base cabinets, while others prefer it to be slightly to definitely lower.

Depending on the size and complexity of the project, you can purchase the cabinets and countertops from the home center store and install them — if you don't already have one in place. Otherwise, the services of a remodeler, carpenter, handyman, kitchen and bath designer, or interior designer will be required.

Up-Front Controls

This is one area where you can really make life easier, more convenient, and safer for everyone in your home.

Certain appliances already are created with their operating controls and digital displays mounted on their front panels so that you don't have to stretch to reach them or strain to see the settings — front-loading washing machines, automatic dishwashers, microwave ovens, ranges, and induction and other cooktops are examples of this.

Many other appliances and fixtures (such as clothes dryers, laundry sinks, garbage disposals, range hoods, and exhaust fans) can be switched out for ones more accessible when it comes time to replace them, and you can do this or use a remodeler, handyman, or appliance installer to do this.

Some of the changes will require moving or adding switches, gas lines, or plumbing, and an electrician or plumber may need to get involved also.

Easy-Access Appliances

Many kitchen and other appliances have great solutions already available — front-loading washing machines, refrigerators, microwave ovens, cooktops, ranges, and dishwashers. Others need to be selected or installed with universal design and accessibility in mind.

Most, but not all, front-loading automatic clothes washing machines have the controls and the door located on the front so that anyone can use it. It can even be raised with a pedestal base if it needs to be a little higher for members of the household. There are a few front-loading machines with controls at the back.

A top loading washing machine does not provide these advantages — even if the controls are on the front. The door is on top and must be pulled up to open it. The controls typically are at the back and require reaching to access them. Then the clothes must be lifted to be placed into the machine, while the wet clothes must be lifted from the machine to dry them. These require good hand and arm strength and range-of-motion. Shorter people are going to have some difficulty with access. People using a wheelchair or other mobility assistance will have no access. Frequently you have to lean over the machine to make sure that all of the items have been retrieved.

Refrigerators come in two styles that offer great accessibility — the side-by-side and the french-door models. In the french-door style with two doors (often equally sized) that close to the middle and open outward in either direction, the top shelves are going to be harder for someone short, seated, or with limited range-of-motion to reach.

However, there are models available with either two separate bottom drawers or with a drawer within a drawer. Often one of these drawers has the option of serving as a refrigerator compartment in addition to being set as a freezer. Set to the refrigerator mode, access would be available for people unable to reach higher shelves in the refrigerator.

Water and ice in the door are a great feature that saves opening the door. Some models have a small access door on the right side that can be opened easily also.

Some cooktops have the controls on the surface along the front edge or in the lower corner of them.

Induction cooktops have the touch controls along the front edge but on the surface of the cooktop.

Ranges (gas and electric) have their controls on the front facing out so they are easily accessible, and some knobs are actually red — totally or with accents.

Dishwashers are accessible to all — either the traditional model with the door opening down and the pull-out baskets or the newer style with two drawers that open independently. They work well for someone short, seated, or in a wheelchair also.

As for appliances that need to be selected or installed with accessibility and safety in mind, the oven when it is part of a range is fine (but the broiler part is often too low). When the oven is mounted in the wall apart from the stove or range, it needs to be at a useable height to facilitate access and safe use. Remember that very hot foods are coming out of the oven.

Finding and selecting an oven with a side-opening door (hinged along the side rather than the bottom) provides more safety, convenience and accessibility than one that opens down. Just be aware of extra clearance that may be required for the door to open safely and what access may be blocked temporarily by the open door.

For double ovens (or separate microwave and wall oven units mounted vertically over each other), the top unit tends to be quite high for many people. Care should be taken to lower it and to make sure the controls and display are at eye-level or below.

Many newer clothes dryers have the controls mounted on the front, but some still have them at the back.

Ideally, locate the washer and dryer so that the doors close toward each other (opposing). This way, you can take clothes from the washer and put them right into the dryer without moving much or at all. Keep in mind the access and maneuvering room that might be required to safely use these appliances.

Microwaves are often mounted in line with the cabinets over the range. They typically have a range hood/exhaust fan function built into them also.

Because of where they are installed, it is difficult for many people to reach and use them or see the controls well due the height of them — especially when they have to reach over a stove or cooktop that could be in use.

People who are short, or those with range-of-motion or arm strength issues, face the additional challenge of removing hot food from the microwave and trying to set it down safely.

Some microwaves are installed with them directly resting on the countertop. While this brings them to a very useable and accessible level, countertop space is often forfeited.

As for range hoods, look for ones with a remote control that can operate the exhaust fan and the task lights that often are a part of them no matter how high they are installed — or have a switch for each (fan and lights) installed on the front edge of the countertop.

Many homeowners and renters can replace appliances on their own or with the help of an installer from the store where the appliances are purchased. Some professional assistance might be needed from a plumber, handyman, remodeler, or interior designer.

Easy-Access Faucets

In addition to having user-friendly and accessible appliances in your kitchen, bathrooms, and laundry room — including up-front controls — another universal design feature that goes along with this strategy is having the water faucets near the front of the sink or countertop. However, this isn't always practical or desirable.

They can't look awkward and out-of-place suggesting that they are only there because someone has difficulty reaching them in their traditional location at the back of the sink — even though they may be much safer to use and access from this location.

Also, there may not be sufficient room to install the faucet due to the space required for the water supply lines — particularly in kitchens. This may interfere with adjacent cabinets and simply be impractical.

For kitchen or bathroom sinks (or pedestal or wall-hung sinks) that come with the holes already punched or formed into them in the traditional position at the back of the sink, this strategy of moving them forward and along the left or right side of the sink toward the front just would not work.

For bathroom vessel sinks and kitchen integrated bowl sinks where there is sufficient room to the side of the bowls to run water supply lines without encroaching on adjacent cabinets, however, a forward located single-lever faucet along either side of the bowl can be a good universal design feature for access and ease of use.

The water supply lines will need to be wrapped or boxed-in under the sink to keep people from bumping into them since they are in a location different than where people normally expect them to be.

For laundry sinks and sinks on islands, this strategy of locating the faucets along the side and toward the front increases access to the faucets since these sinks tend to be deeper (as is the case with the laundry sink) or located farther back from the front of the countertop (as is often true with island sinks).

Wall Blocking

Wall blocking by itself — adding dimensional lumber (2" x 6", 2" x 8", 2" x 10", or 2" x 12" boards even though the 2" inch dimension is really only 1½" and the other dimensions are somewhat smaller also) horizontally and flush between the vertical wall studs to provide material into which to anchor a future installation of grab bars or other devices — is not a universal design strategy.

However, it is an adaptable strategy that will facilitate the later installation of towel bars, grab bars, or other items that need to be anchored securely to the wall without being concerned about locating a stud or working with products that may not fit exactly where the studs are located. This increases safety since the objects can be mounted more securely, irrespective of where the mounting holes are. It also eliminates the need to rely on wall fasteners.

Using wider boards (say a 10" or 12" board versus a 6" one) provides more flexibility in choosing an appropriate mounting height.

Using plywood sheathing (⅝" or ¾") across the studs will work, but it less than half as thick as 2" lumber (again, normally 1½" although labeled as 2") and reduces the functional size of the room by its thickness since the drywall needs to go on top of it rather than applied directly to the wall studs.

Windows

Every home has windows, but there's a lot more to consider than just having them. This is an area of your home that often goes unnoticed or overlooked in a remodeling project, but it is extremely important for many reasons — safety, comfort, security, peace-of-mind, and convenience, for instance.

Replacing windows is a task for the professional carpenter, contractor, window installer, or remodeler.

People generally select their home in part by the size and location of windows. They look for how well the windows add natural light to a space and how that varies throughout the day, the ability of the windows to provide ventilation and fresh air when they are opened, the view the windows offer from various rooms, how the windows might suggest furniture placement in a room (in a bedroom, family room, living room, dining room, or kitchen), and the way the size and shape of the windows fit into the exterior design.

Windows generally come with the home and are not specifically selected for how accessible they are or how easy they are to open. This often isn't discovered until after living in the home with your own furniture in place where you normally use it. Some windows are not as accessible or easy to open as might have been thought once cabinetry or furniture is in front of them

— partially blocking them or creating a barrier to reaching them.

Also, how far someone might need to reach, how much hand and arm strength they may need, or the range-of-motion required to raise or lower the window sash or operate the crank are additional considerations that may not immediately come to mind. In fact, discomfort or injury can result from trying to access and operate stubborn windows.

Depending on what your local building codes require as a minimum height of a window from the floor, windows that provide easy viewing through them from a seated position are at a good height for everyone. At such a height, anyone can access them as well for egress in an emergency and for emergency personnel to gain entry. This attribute of windows is often overlooked.

Thus, a relatively low window — in terms of distance of the sill from the floor — is a universal design feature because anyone can approach it and see through the glass (even from a seated position) and observe what is happening outside or enjoy the view.

The lower the windows are in relation to the floor, the easier they are going to be to open, but it's not just a matter of reaching the crank or the sash. For safety, security, peace-of-mind, and comfort, the window sash needs to be latched securely.

For casement windows, the latch that secures the windows is usually located along the side of the window. However, try to find and select windows with the latch near the bottom or actually along the bottom rather than halfway up the side of the sash.

You can also find casement windows where the handle that secures them just turns 90° to unlatch them. There is nothing to turn or crank in or out. Once unlatched, the windows simply push out or pull it to open them.

Contrast this with single-hung and double-hung windows where the latching/locking mechanism is on top of the lower window sash or frame.

Sometimes security pins can be installed in the sides of the sash by drilling through it and into the frame in one or more places to keep the window from opening or to keep it opened securely at a pre-determined amount — effectively bypassing the lock at the top of the lower sash and making it easier to use.

Depending on the size of the windows, how high they are installed from the floor, how heavy they are, and how difficult they are to open and close, a short person, a child, someone in a wheelchair, someone with range-of-motion issues in their upper body, or someone without a lot of hand and arm strength or abdominal muscle strength may be unable to release or operate the windows.

So, pay attention to the actual operation of opening and closing the window once they are unlatched or unpinned — the ease or difficulty in turning the crank to open a casement window or the physical act of raising or closing the lower sash of a single- or double-hung window.

You may decide to replace your single- or double-hung windows if you have them and use only casement windows — a solid window panel framed by wood, wood with vinyl cladding, or aluminum that opens on a pivot horizontally or vertically, depending on the style selected.

This will eliminate reaching and range-of-motion concerns for opening and closing the windows.

Whatever you select, make sure they are lightweight yet durable and that you and others in your home can operate them easily and safely.

Adding impact resistance glass will be beneficial and universal also for safety, security, and convenience — and peace of mind against possible intruders, mischief, vandalism, or wind storms.

Spiral Stairways

If you have a home that was built with a spiral staircase or stairway — possibly used to access your master bedroom, a loft, a library, or a den while keeping the footprint of the staircase to a minimum, you may find that the stairway is now very difficult to use.

It may have been practical at one time, but now you find using it is not something you like doing.

They are narrow and wind from the bottom to the top. Anyone with balance issues, range-of-motion limitations in the hips or legs, a bad back, sore feet, joint issues, or poor stamina would not be able to use the spiral stairway effectively.

One solution is to remove the spiral stairway and replace it with a pneumatic tubular elevator that fits in roughly the same space and sits right on the main floor. You can stand or sit in the elevator as it moves between floors.

It can go through the ceiling where the spiral staircase is. For a loft or bridge area, the tubular elevator can go along side it without needing to go through the floor.

Regular Stairways & Lifts

If you have a two-story home or more, or one with a basement, you have stairs. You might also have an elevator, but you have stairs.

As long as we aren't talking about a winding grand central staircase that has no walls along its sides, there are ways to adapt stairways to make them accessible to anyone — in place or in addition to using the stairs. However, no one is suggesting removal of the stairs. They still remain.

There are chair lifts (for people who can sit in a chair while it moves them up and down stairs), platform lifts (for people who can remain sitting in their wheelchair or standing with their walker), and elevators (that can move people between floors).

An electric outlet located at the base of the stairs and the landing — even if not required by the building code — will mean that a chair lift could be installed at a future date if necessary or desired. In the meantime, one can never have too many outlets. An outlet located here would facilitate plugging in decorative holiday lights and using the vacuum or other electrical appliances in this area of the home.

Just make sure with any type of remodeling that is done on or around the base of the stairs that sufficient floor space is maintained to accommodate the chair lift track. It rests on the floor and extends well past the base of the stairs — creating a potential tripping hazard if there is a walkway or hallway there.

Lifts and elevators are not universal designs because they are a visible improvement to the home for a specific use. Nevertheless, they can be used and accessed by many people — those in your home as well as guests, and others with minor discomforts that enjoy the assistance to those with more severe limitations that actually require it. They provide a safe way of moving between floors for people who need the help.

Regardless, for general safety and comfort, make sure that all stairs are fully enclosed (the treads and the risers). Many basements steps are open along the back — allowing the possibility that someone might twist their ankle or catch their foot (and then fall) by sticking their foot into the open space.

Also, you want sure, safety footing on the stair treads themselves to prevent someone from slipping on them.

Dumbwaiters/Clothes Chute

This is a little like an elevator for items and articles that need to be transported between floors (in multi-story or basement homes). As long as it is installed so that it is at an accessible height, it is a great universal design feature.

Rather than carrying items up and down stairs — for those who might have limited strength or holding power, those with balance or coordination issues, those with poor stamina, or those using assistance — this is a great solution.

Simply put the items in the dumbwaiter car and send them up or down to the next level. They can even remain on the car until someone goes up or down a floor to retrieve them from the car later.

They don't have a particularly large footprint, but some construction is going to be involved in installing this. A remodeler, contractor, occupational therapist, kitchen and bath designer, DME provider, and electrician are resources for you.

A similar idea to the dumbwaiter — but one without moving parts — is the clothes chute. This feature has been around for years — again for multiple story homes or basement homes.

The principle of this feature is that clothes, after they have been worn or used (such as towels and linens) are dropped into the clothes chute for a direct ride to the laundry room (on the first floor or basement) — depending on where the washing machine is located. Gravity is the engine for this, and it only works for moving items downward.

First-Floor Master Suite

If your home is multi-level and does not have a bedroom of some type on the main floor, you should consider creating a first floor master suite. The market is very receptive to this idea so this will aid in resale when it comes time for that as well as being a practical addition to your home now.

Even if you and everyone else in your home are able to climb stairs without difficulty, or you plan on installing a lift or elevator (or you already have done so), there are many times when you or someone else (even a visiting relative or houseguest) might benefit from a first floor master bedroom — even if this is not the main place you or they sleep. Occasional illnesses, surgeries, or injuries might make a main floor bedroom easier to use or more comfortable than going to their normal bedroom.

This is going to require professional help to accomplish — especially to make sure a bathroom is connected to the bedroom. The space layout for the remainder of the main floor may have to change as well to accommodate the first-floor master suite.

Depending on the available space on the main floor and the ability to convert a den or study into a bedroom, this is likely a major undertaking. However, this is a safety, comfort, convenience, and accessible strategy.

Two Master Suites

Years ago, many homes were built with just one bathroom for the entire home so these layouts did not have a master suite or ensuite with a private bathroom just for use by the master bedroom.

If your home does not have a master suite that includes a bathroom that you don't have to share with the rest of the home, that would be a great place to start in your remodeling.

Then we can consider adding a second master suite. When adult children visit (or move back in), they can use it. If a sibling, parent, or other relative visits or moves in with you, it will accommodate them — the same with other visiting houseguests. A visiting or live-in housekeeper or caregiver could use it also.

When minor illnesses, insomnia, post-surgery recovery, or other issues affect you or someone else in your family, it may be desirable to have separate quarters where you or they can retreat to and have privacy.

This may not be a high priority item on your list of remodeling projects, but it is universal and will add value to your home. Obviously this is a major construction project that will require the services of several professionals to accomplish.

Garage Access

In homes with an attached garage, there is a step-up from the garage floor to the main floor of your home. It might be a relatively small 4"-6" step up, or it could be as many as two or three constructed concrete or wooden steps.

Minimizing the impact of this grade differential for people of small stature, or those with range-of-motion, balance, mobility, or other issues will make going from the garage to the home — or from the home into the garage — more comfortable and safe.

The difference in height between the garage floor and the floor of your home may be such that the only way to accommodate the difference is to add a ramp. Then there will need to be plenty of approach room to access the ramp plus a landing area with approach room to open the door to your home from the garage.

If the difference between the two levels is small, a small slope can be framed and poured with concrete to allow access between the two floors without a specific step up or down.

Just make sure the run (length of the slope or small ramp) is long enough to be provide safe footing and eliminate the possible loss of balance in using it. Make sure that this bridge is not slippery.

Back-Up Power

Aside from occasional power outages from various causes, storms can disrupt electricity for brief periods of time — from a few seconds to several hours or days.

While comfort, convenience, accessibility, and safety

are important considerations during a power outage due to such items as alarm systems, lighting (interior and exterior), heating and air conditioning, computers, TVs, appliances, and refrigeration, you might also have some medically necessary equipment that depends on electricity as well.

While fuel oil, propane, or natural gas may normally power some items in your home such as hot water and heating, an electrical outage will shut off lights, TVs, computers, cooling, and refrigerators — at a minimum.

Back-up generators are quite useful and universal for supplying electrical power needs when the normal power service is interrupted — they just are not practical for taking over the energy load of running your entire home (for more than a few hours) because of the size of the generator that would be required and the amount of energy required to run it and keep it going.

Generators can power many essential and necessary systems, appliances, and items in your home — just not all of the energy needs in your home without a large capacity generator and a large, limitless, dependable power source such as natural gas (which can get expensive to run your entire house on a generator for several days).

If chair lifts, platform lifts, or elevators are present in your home — or you plan on installing them — they likely have back-up power designed into them. If not, the back-up generator installed for your other energy needs would operate them. Even a UPS (uninterruptible power supply) battery like the one you use for your computer can provide temporary backup for a few uses of a power bed or chair lift.

A back-up generator is something an electrician needs to install along with a remodeler or handyman so that it engages automatically when it is supposed to and powers those systems or devices that are important.

Installing the generator wrong could be an inefficient energy drain by running too many devices (or the wrong circuits) and very dangerous by backflowing power onto the electrical grid.

Indoor Air Quality

Many people suffer from allergies, and there is more attention being paid to indoor air quality — particularly as the building envelop is being designed and created to be tighter. Removing carpeting is a positive strategy for improving indoor air quality because of the way it's made and the way it traps and hold dust and allergens.

Another popular and universal strategy for indoor air quality, general comfort, and ease of breathing is using low- or no-VOC paints, glues, adhesives, and building materials (ones that don't off-gas).

Built-in accents are attractive, but they are dust-catchers and contribute to air quality issues. Niches, bookcases, open beams, large window sills and ledges, decorative columns with fluted surfaces, and many other building accessories and finishes add aesthetically to a home's interior but attract dust or allow dust to settle and remain on them. They aren't always the easiest to vacuum or wipe off either.

I'm not talking about your personal furniture although as you shop for new furniture you might want to keep this in mind. For now just pay attention to design or architectural elements that may have been added to your home and how to keep them clean. You may want to remove some of them.

A cleaner, easier-to-maintain look will promote better indoor air quality (while possibly sacrificing some aesthetic treatments). Determine if there are design elements in your home that seem to be unusual dust catchers or those that might be hard to reach and clean. Also, keep this in mind when designing future improvements.

General Clutter

This is not a matter of design or furnishings specifically, but keeping our homes free of clutter and potential tripping or stumbling hazards is a major safety emphasis.

I have talked about glare, contrast, and busyness in patterns and designs. General clutter is something we need to keep in mind and keep it in check as well.

While collecting mementos, souvenirs, and "stuff" along our journey through life helps us relive or revisit happy or milestone moments in our life or remind us of important events, they can get in the way or take over our space if we aren't careful.

Collections, a junk drawer here and there, a jar of buttons or screws, scrapbooks, and the like are found in many homes. It's when we begin hanging onto things that we don't have a proper storage place for or when we have more items than we can reasonably manage to keep organized that we begin facing clutter.

Things lying about, extra furniture pieces that take up more floor space that they should, stack-upon-stack of boxes, closets and other storage spaces filled to capacity, clothes that we will never wear again, mostly empty containers or outdated ones of products we aren't likely to use, or other items that interfere with the general enjoyment and safe use of our homes need to be addressed.

We need to streamline our living spaces for the safety of navigating them, accessibility, visitability, general comfort, convenience, and enjoyment of our homes.

6

Universal Design On The Outside

Why Look At The Exterior?

In addition to all of the improvements, changes, modifications, strategies, and new installations you can make or have done on the inside of your home to increase the universal accessibility, safety, convenience, security, and comfort, there are many safety concerns on the outside as well.

This is true whether you rent or own your home and whether it's a single family detached structure or a semi-attached/detached home such as a duplex, villa, or townhome.

Before you, or someone coming to visit you, ever gets inside your home or apartment, there needs to be safe access and approach on the outside.

The principles of universal design and accessibility don't just magically begin once you or your visitors or guests open the front door and enter your living space.

They begin at the curb and continue along your entry sidewalks and driveway to the front door.

Here are a few ideas and things to keep an eye on to get you started creating an accessible and safe living environment from the outside-in.

Zero-Step/Barrier-Free Entrances

In some parts of the country, building codes may not allow a true zero-step entrance into your home that is at grade level (with no noticeable change from the entrance walk to the main floor of your home).

However, there may other ways to accomplish this through a gentle sloping or ramping that bridges the few inches that the threshold needs to be above grade for flooding concerns or other issues.

Make sure you or your contractor follow the local building codes in terms of what is required or allowed in terms of making a zero-step threshold or entry — even if you don't get a building permit for the work.

The concept of a zero-step or barrier free entry is to allow anyone easy, unrestricted access to your home, whether it's you, other household members, your guests or your visitors (invited or not) — from young to old, with or without mobility assistance (a walker, cane, or wheelchair), being pushed in a baby carriage or stroller, using a wheeled toy, or just having range-of-motion limitations, joint issues, or foot problems that makes stepping up and down difficult.

Everyone will need to step on or over the wooden or metal threshold against which the entry door closes; however, the concept of barrier free is to reduce and eliminate other steps and barriers along the entry walk — from the driveway or street to the entrance of your home.

Even when small changes in grade (steps) can't be totally eliminated because of the building code or physical elements of your yard, they can adapted to minimize their impact.

In some cases, an attractive, well-constructed, and well-landscaped ramp may be used as universal access to your home — or in addition to steps or another type of approach that might be present. A longer ramp will keep the angle of rise (slope) to a minimum and make it more comfortable for anyone to use it.

Well-done ramps can provide an alternative entry without necessarily calling attention to their presence — whether they are required for accessibility or not.

Some jurisdictions consider ramps to be permanent structures that must have a building permit and be inspected. However, most places do not have this requirement so you can design them as you like.

Sidewalks

Many homes are built without much attention to the sidewalks leading from the street to the front door or from the driveway to the front door.

Depending on the age of the neighborhood and whether it was built as part of a master plan or homes were built one-at time over the years, this reflects how or if sidewalks are used to access the front door.

Some homes have walkways or sidewalks connecting the public sidewalk that is near and parallel to the street with the front door or entry stoop in a straight line. Some use a walkway that is curved. Some have the connecting walkway from the driveway to the entrance without any connection to the public walkway. Some home are built in neighborhoods with no public sidewalks.

Sometimes a basic walkway is formed and poured — or one is created with brick pavers or stepping stones (concrete pavers) — without much attention to function. Sometimes there is no formal sidewalk — just have a path, with or without stepping stones.

The dirt path can become muddy, and those with stepping stones can become overgrown with grass and difficult to use because of the spacing between them or the fact that they are broken or pitched in various directions. Twisting ankles from stepping on the stones unevenly is a big risk.

Many dirt paths and hard surface sidewalks retain water during a rain or lawn sprinkling, and some walkways have intermediate steps and may or may not have railings for assistance.

A much more strategic, accessible, and visitable approach to designing a sidewalk is to make it wide enough for easy use for children playing, for people using a walker or wheelchair, for moving furniture or equipment in and out of the home, or for two or more people to walk side-by-side (either going along together or coming and going in opposite directions) on the walkway.

Also take into account creating a non-slip surface (under most conditions), the rise and slope of the walkway (eliminating steps whenever possible), installing it slightly above grade for better drainage (if the building code allows it) but not so high as to become a tripping or stumbling issue when approaching it from the side, and making it easy to use in terms of twists and turns. Depending on its length, there might even need to be one or more flat intermediate landings along it.

Designing, forming, pouring, and finishing your walkway is something for the professionals to do — landscape architect, flatwork contractor, cement finisher, remodeler, occupational therapist, architect, or handyman.

Remember to include radiant heating in your sidewalk remodeling plans unless you are in a warm climate.

Ramps

Ramps are not purely a universal design element because they do have a relatively large footprint and aren't unobtrusive — they are quite visible unless strategically incorporated into the landscaping design.

This does not mean that they can't be used by everyone, however. Nearly anyone of any age or ability can walk or use assistance to get themselves up and down a ramp unless.

In most local jurisdictions, ramps are not governed by building or zoning codes. Therefore, you can build or use what you like. Be sure to check before beginning, however, because they are regulated in some places.

Ramps generally provide safe access for someone with difficulty in climbing steps, negotiating changes in elevation, or for anyone using mobility assistance such as a cane, walker, or wheelchair.

If you need to install a ramp specifically for yourself or others in your home, you can participate in the size, length, shape, and location of it — even if you create a new entranceway into your home just for the ramp.

Consider the length of time the ramp likely will need to be used (use your best guess, or design it for several years if you aren't sure). This will help you select the appropriate materials to use and might also factor into where you decide to locate it. The next owner of your home may appreciate having it also — especially if it's designed well and attractively landscaped.

This might be the primary entrance into your home or a secondary one — depending on where you place it and how you design it. It could replace an existing walkway or be used in addition to it.

It can blend into your overall landscaping by placing a hedge, bushes, a planter, or a knee wall (brick, stone, stucco, or siding to match your home) along the ramp on the side visible from the street to create a more unobtrusive look that just fits in. This will also add a little more privacy for those using the ramp.

Remember to follow the appropriate guidelines for the slope of the ramp (even though this is not a requirement in most cases) and to install curbing, sides of some type, a lower secondary railing, and some type of transition (appropriate for the surface, such as a rubber insert, sanded treads, sandblasting, or etching) at each end of the ramp to aid in traction.

Depending on your skill level and ability, you might be able to create this, but it is likely that you will require professional assistance to complete it.

Tree Branches & Landscaping

Landscaping is a great accent to beautify and personalize the outsides of our homes. It can include annual, perennial, and seasonal flowers, shrubs, succulents such as cactus, bushes, and trees (fruit bearing or flowering, or not). Depending on your climate, you may have color throughout the year or only during the more temperate months — not counting evergreens.

Since we are concerned with safety, it's important to plant flowers, bushes, and shrubs so that they do not interfere with safe passage or usage along any of your walkways or patio areas. Pay particular attention to sharp, stiff, or thorny plants and branches that might stab, puncture, scratch, or otherwise injure or cause discomfort to someone who veered from or fell off the sidewalk or patio.

Tree branches that overhang sidewalks, porches, and entrances must be high enough to provide shade and not interfere with someone walking under them. If trees or large bushes are planted so close to sidewalks or driveways that their low hanging or drooping branches might allow someone to walk into them or hit their head — or dropped branches, fruit, berries, seeds, and leaves create a slippery or tricky footing issue — trim or remove the offending plants to restore a safe passageway. This could be an on-going maintenance issue.

Entry Steps/Stoop/Porch

Each home is different as far as how someone approaches the front door and accesses it. Homes are often somewhat similar in a given neighborhood because of when or by whom they were built, however.

The concern with the concrete pad or stoop outside the front door or the wooden or poured concrete porch is that it must provide safe footing and enough access room and maneuverability for people to approach the front door and open it or allow it to be opened for them to pass through it.

If you have a small stoop that is 3' x 3' or similar, this generally is not large enough for someone to open the storm door outward and get out of the way of it. It's even more of a challenge for someone using a wheelchair, cane, or walker — and someone may have balance issues also.

Pay particular attention to how the stoop or porch is protected. Often, there are no railings to keep someone from failing off the sides of the surface. This is a significant safety risk.

It's important from a safety, comfort, and convenience standpoint to have a porch, front patio, landing area, approach zone, stoop, or pad at the front door that is large enough to allow more than one person to gather while waiting for you or someone else in your home to open the door for them and also allow them to maneuver out of the way of the door opening out (for entrance doors that might open out and for screen or storm doors).

To exit and leave your home — whether it's you, someone else in your household, or a visitor or guest — the same is true. People walk out the door and then stop to make sure they have everything with them that they are supposed to before going on their way.

Make sure that the surface of your patio, stoop, or porch provides sufficient traction to keep you, your family, and your guests or visitors from slipping during inclement weather.

Entry steps, when they are present — whether it's just a minor step up from the sidewalk onto the stoop or patio (or step down going the other way) or several steps, wooden or concrete — create their own safety, comfort, convenience, visitability, and accessibility issues. They are not universal because there are many people who cannot use them safely — or at all.

You will need to look at safe alternatives for your entrance steps if you currently have them. This should be a relatively high priority for your personal safety and those of people who visit you.

Seek the assistance of professionals to help you design and create a safer, more accessible entryway.

Entry Shelves/Tables/Furniture

A universal design strategy that definitely appeals to all ages and abilities and addresses safety, comfort, convenience, and accessibility issues is an outdoor entry shelf or piece of furniture such as a table.

This is installed or placed next to the entrance (the latch side or door handle side of the front door — unless you use the side door or back door as much or more than the front door and it can apply to these doors also).

This is another reason for having a large enough stoop, patio, or porch at your entrance.

The shelf, table, stand, or other piece of furniture should be somewhat lower in height than the door handle so as not to interfere with its function and safe operation. You can use most any dimension that you like, but it should be large enough and deep enough to be functional without be so big that it is obtrusive or a barrier to entering safely.

Depending on its size and shape, it might provide storage space inside or underneath it or allow for a small sculpture or plant on top.

It can be wood or metal and can be painted, stained, or decorated as you like to be compatible with the general design, theme, and colors of your home or entry porch. It can even make a statement.

It's quite common for any of us to get out of the car and walk up to the front door with our hands full of various things — whether it's our home or we are calling on someone .

This may not be an all-the-time occurrence, but often you might be carrying the mail, an umbrella (open or closed), a jacket that you aren't wearing, groceries, packages, shopping bags, books, tools, dry cleaning, a briefcase, purse, small children, a cup of coffee or a soft drink, fast food (that you are still eating or in the bag to eat once inside), or a cell phone.

Maybe you are trying to assist someone else to get into your home or show attention to a pet that greets you.

Then, with your hands full of what you are carrying or attending to, you need to look for your keys, make or take a phone call, keep from dropping something you have been carrying that is beginning to slip, or have a hand free to open the door.

Even if you aren't driving but are simply bringing in the mail or things from the yard, the shelf can be helpful.

Having a shelf or object (such as a table or stand) to set things on makes perfect sense rather than juggling them, trying to balance them, setting them on the ground, or dropping them.

Just make sure that whatever you decide to use — a shelf, cabinet, stand, table, or other object or piece of furniture —that it is painted or otherwise treated to withstand precipitation if it is in an area that might get wet (directly or from windblown rain or snow).

If you use a piece of furniture rather than a shelf, be prepared to change it occasionally as it shows signs of wear or you grow tired of it.

Covered Entry/Guttering

When you arrive at your front door — or you have guests or visitors that come to your front door — it should be dry, even if it is snowing or raining right up until you or your guests arrive at the door.

This is a safety, comfort, and convenience solution that definitely appeals to all ages and abilities. You and your guests or visitors need to be sheltered from rain or snow when it is present so you can pause in a dry area immediately before entering your home without being subjected to the precipitation.

This gives you and your visitors time to compose yourself as you shake off the rain or snow, take off your raincoat, clean off your boots or shoes, or shake off and fold up your umbrella — whether you first have to unlock the door or just open it and enter.

Most entrances have an overhang of sorts, but at a minimum guttering should be installed to keep the precipitation from running off the roof and onto you or your guests — generally at a fairly heavy flow — when you or they approach the door.

Guttering also — if it is installed correctly — will collect and drain the water away from the sidewalk or driveway that you and your guests will use to approach the front door — keeping everyone's feet dryer and providing safer, surer footing on the walkway and more accessibility without having to navigate around or through puddles or slippery spots on the walkway.

A covered entry or porch (that also has guttering along the edge of it for the reasons just mentioned) provides even more protection and shelter.

Then with the entry shelf, stand, table, or other piece of furniture I mentioned, you can set down anything you are holding while you open the door.

You might be able to install the guttering that you get from the home center store. However, a covered entry is likely a job for a handyman, carpenter, or remodeler — possibly an architect or roofer if it is particularly large or will be tied into the existing roofline.

Door Closers

The concept of an automatic door closer sounds attractive for people with poor arm strength or range-of-motion that might have difficulty in holding onto a door as they opened it to walk through or in reaching for it to close it — or for those who walk particularly slow or use a cane, wheelchair, or walker.

However, there are a couple of considerations. An automatic door opener while fairly easy to use is not totally a universal design element.

Small children could activate the door just to see it open, and someone close to the door but unaware that it was about to open might be struck by it — making this a safety concern.

If the closer is being used because someone is relatively slow on their feet or uses a wheelchair or other mobility assistance such as a walker or cane, the time for the door to remain open would need to be adjusted and set for a longer sequence — again, for safety.

A manual switch to activate the door to return to its closed position is likely the best solution when the door closer serves as an effective solution otherwise.

This is likely something for an electrician, remodeler, or other professionals to install for you.

Radiant Heating

In areas where temperatures are cold enough for ice and snow to be present, a universal design feature and treatment that provides safety, comfort, convenience, and accessibility is radiant heating in the concrete sidewalks (front, back, and side), driveways, entrance stoops, and patios around the home so that the ice and snow are melted and the possibility of slipping or having unsure footing is greatly reduced or eliminated.

Also, this also will keep wet patches of melted snow or ice or other precipitation (rain or sleet) from freezing when the temperature drops low enough.

This obviously is a major renovation project and will require the services of people such as a remodeler, flatwork contractor, HVAC contractor, cement mason, architect, and landscape architect to produce an attractive, effective result.

Unloading/Landing Area

This is a universal design concept that isn't given much thought until there is a need for it.

This definitely applies to nearly every home — those with single-car driveways, ones with normal two-car driveways, and those without a complete solid surface driveway.

For homes with very wide two-car or even three-car driveways (more than just the width of the garage), the driveways possibly can accommodate people unloading from a vehicle without stepping in the grass, dirt, or planting area along the sides of the driveway, and no other work may be desired or required to improve the loading or unloading experience.

For the rest of the driveways, however, this universal design treatment should be implemented.

Generally, being able to unload a car, van, or truck (yours or someone visiting you) from the passenger side onto a hard surface would only be possible if the vehicle was parked to the extreme left side of the driveway with the right side being used for the loading and unloading area.

This is why this loading and unloading activity doesn't work at all — and isn't particularly safe — for single-car driveways.

For increased safety, convenience, comfort, visitability, and accessibility, the driveway — regardless of its current width (but definitely for single-car and normal two-car driveways) — should be enlarged along the right side of the driveway (facing it from the street) with a hard, all-weather surface of concrete or pavers to allow plenty of firm footing for all passengers to disembark from their vehicle (wherever it is parked on the driveway) and to allow plenty of space for all items in the vehicle to be unloaded, including a walker or wheelchair when that is the case.

This extra loading and unloading space is beneficial for everyone — especially on inclement days or when the vehicle needs to be loaded or unloaded with luggage, supplies, pets, boxes, or other objects in addition to the occupants of the vehicle. Think of unloading groceries, home improvement supplies, sporting goods, or other items after an afternoon of shopping, soccer or baseball practice, and running errands.

For vans with ramps that extend from the vehicle (to allow people in wheelchairs or those with other mobility issues to safely enter and exit the vehicle), there needs to be space for the ramp to deploy and have it rest on a hard surface.

Everything that holds true for you and your family as far as using the driveway safely for loading and unloading or entering and exiting vehicles would also apply to visitors and guests.

If anyone living in home or visiting as a houseguest should need the services of a private van or bus service to go to the doctor or be transported other places, there wouldn't be any concern about where the van or bus parked in the driveway because there would still be a hard-surface approach access.

When the approach area is not needed for passenger unloading or loading, the extra driveway space can be used for accessing your front door, parking (cars, motorcycles, golf carts, or bicycles), as a place to wash your car, as a seating area with lawn chairs, or as a relatively clean play area for children.

You've likely seen other people who have added an additional parking area onto their driveway for additional vehicles, but this is a universal design strategy that accommodates the parking t but primarily exists for the safety, comfort, convenience, visitability, and accessibility of you and your guests.

If you like. you can add landscaping (flowers, mulch, and bushes) around the landing area to give the rain a place to drain and make it look more like an integral feature of your home and less like an afterthought.

This extra width can be just as practical when not needed for getting in and out of the vehicles which is why this is a universal design and visitable strategy.

Think of how your visitors are going to respond to this if they need the extra space to enter or leave their vehicle.

Be sure to include radiant heating in this also because sure footing is very important for this feature.

Lighting

I have already mentioned and discussed photo cells, timers, and motion sensors.

These all work outside as well as indoors provided they can withstand the elements or are used in a relatively dry or covered area (such as on a porch or covered entry, or under the eaves or overhang).

Another type of lighting (in a variety of sizes and styles) that can be used outdoors — anywhere you desire it for security, comfort, peace-of-mind, and general appearance — is a solar powered one.

It can be a yard or house light — utilitarian or decorative — that stays on all night or one that just comes on when it detects motion — depending on what type of light is selected and what the objective is.

The principal advantage to this type of light is that it can be located anywhere on the property because it does not need to be wired into or plugged into electricity.

It draws its energy from batteries that are recharged by the sun.

Of course, the solar collector that recharges the batteries needs to be in a place where it can receive sunlight. Over a prolonged cloudy, rainy, or snowy period (a few days or longer) the batteries will drain, but they will recharge once the sun comes back.

Also, locate it away from tree branches or other objects that might block the sunlight from reaching the solar collector.

Yard Sprinklers/Hoses

Yard sprinklers, hoses, and other tools that are used to care for the grass, garden, flowers, and landscaping are not universal design features, but there is a significant safety component here that needs to be addressed. That's why this section is included.

You might not do any outside work around your home such as mowing the grass, edging the walks, keeping a garden, or tending to bushes, shrubs, flowers, and trees.

You may not be able to do it, choose not to do it, or have a service that you use. If you don't do any yardwork, then there isn't much cause for concern on your part.

However, if you do go out in your yard to maintain it, be careful of tripping hazards that arise from pop-up sprinkler heads on your irrigation system, sprinklers that you have deployed that are attached to hoses, hoses that might be lying in the grass (they might be partially concealed), vines that are growing along the ground that can cause tripping, branches that have fallen or that remain after being trimmed or pruned, and tools that may not have been picked up that might be partially hidden in the grass or landscaping.

Maintaining your yard needs to be done with a focus on safety.

7

Summary Of Universal Design For Safety

Universal Design Makes A Positive Difference

We have been looking at universal design and related options, ideas, treatments, improvements, fixes, and solutions that are available for you to use in renovating your home and adding to the overall safety, comfort, accessibility, convenience, visitability, sustainability, security, and enjoyment of your home.

Anyone who lives in your home, as well as those who visit occasionally or regularly — briefly for an hour or two or for several days or even weeks at a time — should be able to appreciate and enjoy the way you have made your home safer and easier to use. They won't necessarily know specifically what you have or where you have made changes, but they will know that your home is more accessible and comfortable than others they have visited — or perhaps even their own home.

Remember that a key objective in universal design is to make the changes and treatments as invisible as possible so that they don't stand out or call attention to themselves except as something high tech, modern, contemporary, functional, or interesting to use.

In addition to quality improvements that you and the people who visit you get to see and experience in your home, universal design changes and treatments also add value to your home that you will realize when you go to sell it in the future.

Without an appraisal, there is no way to put a specific dollar amount on how much the value of your home will be improved with your universal design changes, but the fact that it literally will appeal to the broadest of audiences makes it generally desirable and worth more. It likely will sell quicker as a result.

Universal Design For Safety

This text has been looking at ways people can be safer living in their homes, or receiving visitors in their homes, with universal design as the primary vehicle or strategy for doing this — regardless of anyone's age, physical size, abilities, strength, range-of-motion, dexterity, coordination, or any other factors that normally might limit or restrict how well someone is able to function within a living space.

As a design emphasis, universal design facilitates and enables changes, improvements, solutions, and treatments that eliminates unsafe conditions or issues and makes your home more comfortable, convenient, visitable, accessible, and secure home for you and those who share your home with you.

Universal design elements allow you and anyone else who lives in your home along with you, or those who visit you (from just dropping by, to a weekly or occasional get-together, to houseguests staying for a few days, to visiting relatives of several days or longer, to parents or in-laws who may stay with you for several weeks or even months at a time) to experience comfortable, safe, accessible, intuitive, easy-to-use design choices in such facets of your home as lighting, controls, doors, cabinets, mirrors, faucets, shelving, appliances, countertops, entrances, walkways, passageways, flooring, and bathroom fixtures.

However, if you have additional safety concerns beyond what I have discussed in this text, consult an occupational therapist, physical therapist, DME (durable medical equipment) consultant, interior designer, kitchen and bath designer, or remodeling contractor.

Universal Design Adds Value And Enjoyment

Whether the universal design changes in and around your home are made by you as the homeowner or tenant, or you call in or consult professionals to manage or accomplish the work, those strategies and solutions will make your life easier and more enjoyable. Your home and living space will be safer to use.

Safety — along with universal design components and strategies — has been our objective in this book.

By making your living space — inside and out — safer and more universal, you will be increasing the level of comfort, convenience, and accessibility in your living environment while reducing the potential for injury, frustration, or unnecessary effort.

You also will be adding to the present and future value of your home in many ways.

In the present, you, and the others in your home (and your visitors and houseguests), will have an easier time of seeing, reaching, and using various controls, fixtures, and appliances. Your home will be much more pleasant and enjoyable to live in and use. It will have a comfort level and convenience factor that is not there — or only partially there (depending on which universal design features you might already have).

By making the changes and modifications that have been discussed and presented, as well as employing the various universal design solutions, strategies, and concepts, the longer term benefit will be the increased or added value of your home in terms of desirability and resale potential for future owners.

Your home should be much more attractive to potential buyers because the changes you make will increase the appeal of your home and broaden the eligible audience interested in purchasing your home.

As much as you look forward to making or contracting for some, most, or all of the changes to your home that have been presented here (notwithstanding those you may already have done), just think of how much a future owner might like to find a home that already has made these changes for them.

Now, It's Up To You

The universal design concepts, treatments, solutions, tips, recommendations, and strategies that I have presented in this book are intended to be used by you to impact and increase the accessibility, safety, comfort, convenience, value (marketability), and visitability of your living space.

Perhaps you can tackle many of these projects yourself. If not, you now know what can be done and how to talk with professionals who can help you achieve the results that you seek.

Now, it's up to you to determine where you want to begin as you start incorporating these features into your home, apartment, or design projects.

You may already have some of these completed. That's a great start, and now you can add to what's already been done.

Begin to prioritize what you want to do, determine which (if any) of the projects you want to do yourself, and then reach out to professionals who can help you with the rest.

Steve Hoffacker

Steve Hoffacker, AICP, CAASH, CAPS, CGA, CGP, CMP, CSP, MCSP, MIRM, is principal of Hoffacker Associates LLC, based in West Palm Beach, Florida. He is a new home sales trainer and sales and marketing coach for remodelers.

Steve is an award-winning new home sales trainer and coach, commercial real estate broker, marketing consultant, award-winning photographer, best-selling author, blogger, teacher, and salesman.

For more than 30 years, he has helped homebuilders, new home salespeople, remodelers, small business owners, and other professional salespeople to be more visible, competitive, profitable, and effective — and to really enjoy themselves as they pursue their business.

He has embraced the concept of universal design and has given you many examples of how to incorporate them into your existing home — as part of normal maintenance and updating or through a larger scale remodeling project.

He interacts with providers from around North America in his classes and has incorporated many of these treatments into his own home so he speaks from practical experience.

Many of the suggestions Steve provides in this book are printed here for the first time. You won't find them anywhere else as of this printing.